UpLevel Your Communication

Compassion in communication has been proven vital in creating a successful business environment, particularly in employee retention and in creating a culture which values and benefits from the contributions of its team. What Dr. Miluna Fausch has accomplished with her clear-eyed yet heartfelt book is an assemblage of mindsets, thought processes, and simple but powerful actions gleaned from her multifaceted experiences as an actor, singer, performer, and corporate coach. This book should be required reading for any manager, boss, or corporate executive who needs to UpLevel their communication skills with compassion, clarity, and professionalism.

Lisa Popeil
Voiceworks®, Los Angeles, CA

UpLevel Your Communication by Dr. Miluna Fausch is an insightful look into how we can bring our hearts into our communication to make our stage presence and command of the room more credible and meaningful. Dr. Fausch shares her own harrowing interactions around a personal medical issue that caused her to come face to face with the ways professionals can marginalize and disrespect people, albeit unintentionally. She then proceeds to share a wealth of wisdom, best practices, and practical suggestions around how we can communicate with candor, intentionality, and compassion in all situations, in ways that are appropriate to our topic and audience. I highly recommend balancing your knowledge and research into communication by reading this thoughtful treatise on harnessing our sensitivity to humanity to deepen our connection with our audiences and dramatically transform how we speak and how we are received.

Rebecca Linquist
Speech coach and American accent expert, English by the Hour

Finally, a guide full of timeless wisdom and clear direction for aware leaders who know that "conscious communication" is everything in today's world. Indeed, our increased reliance on and use of technology in the "Information Age" of the twentieth century has not improved our ability to communicate with one another—in fact, quite the opposite. Humanity must learn to significantly refine our process of communication with one another, and realize that doing so may help us connect holistically and come together to effectively solve the problems of the future. Dr. Miluna Fausch's book is exactly what is needed now—for those who are considered the leaders of today and for those who will become the leaders of tomorrow. Let Dr. Miluna guide us into the next "Age of Clear and Conscious Communication."

Ava Park
Founder, The Museum of Woman

In this deeply personal and perceptive book, Dr. Miluna Fausch will help you find your voice. In the hierarchy of human connection, rhetoric—in the classical sense, "the art of persuasion"—is certainly at the top. If we want to change our culture, we need to change our conversation. This book provides the tools to enable you to communicate in a "clear, charismatic, courageous, and mature" voice ("mature," there's a word you don't hear much in today's polarized culture). Former President Lyndon Johnson used to say, "Let us reason together." Get comfortable, crack open this book, and you can reason with Dr. Fausch as she improves your communication, a vital skill which we could all amplify to better our world.

Ronald J. Baker
Host, *The Soul of Enterprise: Business in the Knowledge Economy*
Founder, VeraSage Institute
Author of the best-selling book, *Implementing Value Pricing: A Radical Business Model for Professional Firms*

Dr. Miluna is a creative and compassionate leader with insight into voice that not only helps us communicate effectively but inspires us to use our voice to make the world a better place.

Vanessa Russell
Founding Executive Director, Love Never Fails

How you sound is such an important part of communication. The tools Dr. Miluna Fausch provides can turn a person's speaking voice from plain, flat, and uninspiring to one that commands the stage and that people want to hear. If your goal is influence, this book is a must.

Mitzi Perdue
Author and businesswoman
Founder, Win This Fight, Stop Human Trafficking Now!

UPLEVEL YOUR

Communication

~

Evolve Your Presence and Speech to
Change Everything

DR. MILUNA FAUSCH
HHCP, PhD

Advantage

Published by Advantage, Charleston, South Carolina.
Member of Advantage Media Group.

ADVANTAGE is a registered trademark, and the Advantage colophon is a trademark of Advantage Media Group, Inc.

Printed in the United States of America.

10 9 8 7 6 5 4 3 2 1

ISBN: 978-1-64225-199-9
LCCN: 2021919986

Book design by Wesley Strickland.

This publication is designed to provide accurate and authoritative information in regard to the subject matter covered. It is sold with the understanding that the publisher is not engaged in rendering legal, accounting, or other professional services. If legal advice or other expert assistance is required, the services of a competent professional person should be sought.

Advantage Media Group is proud to be a part of the Tree Neutral® program. Tree Neutral offsets the number of trees consumed in the production and printing of this book by taking proactive steps such as planting trees in direct proportion to the number of trees used to print books. To learn more about Tree Neutral, please visit **www.treeneutral.com**.

Advantage Media Group is a publisher of business, self-improvement, and professional development books and online learning. We help entrepreneurs, business leaders, and professionals share their Stories, Passion, and Knowledge to help others Learn & Grow. Do you have a manuscript or book idea that you would like us to consider for publishing? Please visit **advantagefamily.com**.

I dedicate this book to my lifetime friend Ava, who taught me how to restore my self-esteem, value my life's work, and know that I had something important to say; and to my husband Reto, who remains my biggest fan.

Contents

In Appreciation

I have so many people who have touched my life, taught me, inspired me, and are now a part of my herstory in some form or another.

Thank you to Source, whom I call Goddess.

To my incredible editing and publishing team at Advantage|ForbesBooks—Harper, Kelly, Jessica, Laura R. and Laura G., Stephanie, Wesley, and Steve.

To Dr. William Slattery III, my rock star neurosurgeon.

To all my friends, teachers, and coaches, who remain too many to list here—you stay in my heart.

To my friends Xuelian, Anne, Barbara, Suresh, Donnie, Pam, Dr. Kris, Donna, Jody, Megan, and Harrilyn.

To my Aunt Donna, who speaks the language of love.

To the memory of Peggy, Pam, my daddy, my mother, my mother-in-law, my father-in-law, Grandma Dorothy, Grandma Maude, Aunt Clyde, and Uncle Hubert.

To my jazz accompanist, Chris, who taught me so much about music and life as we was jammin' on the East Coast.

To Fernanda, who brings as much or more to my life as I bring to hers.

To all my singing teachers, most especially Lisa Popeil.

To my spiritual master teachers—most especially Laurie Grant, Ava Park, Marianne Williamson, Maya White, and Ken Honda.

Thank you to Julia Cameron for birthing *The Artist's Way*.

To my attorney, Jesse; my CPA, Frank; my financial guide, William; my assistant, Valentina; and my bookkeeper, Gina, who are dependable, savvy, wise, kind professionals whom I love to strategize with.

Foreword

Congratulations on selecting UpLevel Your Communication! You are about to commence a life changing journey into upgrading your speech. First let me introduce myself: Frank Mario Castellon, CPA, CGMA, MST, pleasure to meet you. Although my expertise is related to financial matters, my passion is listening to others and helping them resolve complicated financial matters. As you will learn from this book, I practice communication with compassion, respect, and vulnerability. Practicing with this skill set, I developed a successful firm with loyal clients and a group of colleagues I consider my friends. Dr. Miluna Fausch, HHCP, PhD—or as I like to call her, "Dr. M."—and I met in a web conference discussing my favorite subject: taxation. As we talked and shared thoughts, Dr. M. and I bonded as professionals and friends.

As an executive and leader, do you go about your daily life at times wondering if your message is connecting with clients and colleagues? Do you wonder at times if you are viewed as a talking head? When I first entered my profession, I spoke with my brain—analytical, measured, and armored. Communication was a tactical maneuver to accomplish my goals without showing any weakness. In short, a talking head. Dr. M., using her own experiences as well as wit and charm, explains how to communicate to others that "you care about them and their contributions." Using her academic training as a holistic health counselor practitioner (HHCP) and her PhD in holistic psychology, she explains how to speak with compassion and use inclusive language. More importantly, she proposes you open your heart and realize that you will never truly connect with others unless you allow vulnerability. In short, communicate with sensitivity as a human being.

You have a management decision to make—learn effective communication as I did over years of trial and error, or continue reading to learn the language of communicating with compassion, sensitivity, and grace. I invite you, as I did, to turn the pages to commence a life changing journey into upgrading your speech.

My Best,

Frank Mario Castellon,
CPA, CGMA, MST

Where to Begin?

Who could have ever predicted what a paralyzed face and a fist-sized tumor in the right side of my head would do for my life? Who knew that it was, in fact, going to set me on a major detour and road of discovery?

I have been in love with the voice since I was a little girl swinging and singing in my backyard. I could always sing, especially catchy little television commercials, one of my favorites being the Coca-Cola jingle "I'd Like to Teach the World to Sing." I would sing all the TV commercials and couldn't wait for *American Top 40* with that incredible, deep-voiced, perfect-for-radio host Casey Kasem. I dreamed of being a superstar singer or a race car driver.

My purpose in writing this book is to help executives and leaders speak in a voice that is clear, charismatic, courteous, compassionate, courageous, and inclusive! My experience and training include a BS in music business, holistic health counselor practitioner certification, a PhD in holistic psychology, and private training in singing, acting, improvisation, and energy healing. I have performed with my jazz pianist, Chris; sung in operas; acted in theater, television, and film; and written two one-woman cabaret shows.

In one fun commercial we shot, I was riding on a conveyer belt advertising a local cable provider in Maryland. I played a homeless woman on the streets of LA with such realism that people backed away from me. I starred in an independent film where we got to film at places around Washington, DC, including the magnificent Watergate Hotel. I believed that film would make me a star, but it was never finished.

When I doubted my life purpose and wondered whether I could continue as an actor and singer, I found paths of deeper study to add to my talent for teaching voice, acting, and communication. In fact, show business proved to be my best training ground to practice the art of storytelling, convey emotions, and understand human behavior and spoken communication.

So I went back to asking … *What's my purpose?* Where was my love affair with the voice and every aspect of verbal communication going to take me? I had always observed business communication and salespeople and how I was approached either as a cold call or to set up a personal meeting (remember those)? I could see and feel the anxiety, the lack of knowing how to prepare, the ineffectiveness. Plus, I always considered myself a businessperson. My undergraduate degree was in music business, because I understood that it operates as a big business. I came to know that my practice wasn't an either-or but a both.

I was unprepared for the communication style I found when moving to the center of Silicon Valley. It's a different language—male-centric, immature, lacking in eloquence, and aggressive, with no filter or diplomacy. You are expected to take what people dish out. My belief is that there is a huge potential for more beautiful, reverent, uplifting language skills that would inspire and impact people very differently.

So what do I mean by UpLeveling?

- ➴ Upgrading or upskilling

- ➴ Undertaking ownership of what you say and how you say it by using words that have meaning and purpose

- ➴ Feeling joy in the fact that we have the ability to truly lead people and change people by using civil and respectful language

- ➴ Building the necessary self-awareness and emotional availability to move beyond broken relationships, transactional business, and a lack of humanity

How will you move forward as a CEO, as an executive, or as a business owner? Do you understand that your words, intent, and delivery matter? It's important to know that there are people from all over the world who speak different languages and learn in ways different from us. Some people have been injured and gone through trauma. Know that your voice and the way you speak make a difference.

I believe the world has a deep need for true leaders who are mature and move beyond their ego to get to the heart of the matter. The CEOs we will listen to in the future will be those who lead by example with emotional depth, character, candor, and humor.

It's time to stop talking at people instead of with them. It's time to stop using aggressive, bullying language and expecting folks to do what you say simply because you're the boss. The man-child who runs his company like a one-man show has had his day.

I suggest that you read this book in whatever way speaks to you. Perhaps you start with one chapter that applies to your life right now and then continue through the rest of the book. Perhaps you are a reader who starts at the beginning of a book and reads every word. Maybe you will get out the colored markers and Post-it Notes. Do it your way!

My intention is that you read each page with a child's curiosity and an open heart. Writing this book has been one of the most challenging, delicious, and healing times of my life. I threatened to write a book after my surgeries, and then went into a period (seventeen years) when I doubted anyone could benefit from this story. After all, it's *my* story.

I chose to write it myself without the help of a ghost writer (as talented as they are) because I knew this must be written in my own quirky voice. I knew these words needed to be my own and this writing process would (and did) propel me into a deeper healing of my body, mind, emotions, and spirit.

The satisfaction of completion and my story now shared with you is an honor and a blessing, and I look forward to meeting each of you and personally signing your copy of my book (OK, it may be a virtual meeting).

Each chapter in this book begins with a quote from me, along with true stories from my life and ten years of coaching conscientious, high-performing leaders from around the globe. There are case studies and stories of deep transformation sharing why communication matters followed by invitations and questions for you to ask yourself.

I invite you to UpLevel your communication, upgrade your speech, and practice a whole new way of communicating because the leaders who evolve their communication will begin to benefit other people and help change the world! The stakes are high, and folks with staying power are the ones who will shine.

I know from experience that when you choose to speak and express with awareness and thought, your whole life will change. Communication that went beyond my physical speech saved my life. Communicating clearly with the medical system and advocating for my own health forever shifted my understanding of how much it mattered.

I am delighted to reveal that you have it in your ability to bring the art and science of beautiful communication to the world with your unique voice and presence.

Let's get started! Head on over to chapter 1 as I turn back the curtain on my life-will-never-be-the-same medical adventures and first teach you how to communicate with compassion!

Yours truly,

Dr. Miluna Fausch
Monterey, California

Communicating with Compassion

*I never could have predicted what a tumor
in my head would do for my life.*

It seems like a lifetime ago, but there I was sitting in my acting class in Beverly Hills, California. It was 2001, another sunny day in Southern California, because it never rains in Southern California. My husband and I had moved to Los Angeles for my acting career, and that first year it rained exactly three days. I marked those days on my calendar, as I was missing rainy days and lightning and thunderstorms.

I was a student at the Beverly Hills Playhouse in the advanced film scene class. We met three times a week choosing film roles and partners and rehearsing and studying before applying to present our scene before the entire class. I chose a scene from *Fatal Attraction*, the film starring Glenn Close as Alex Forrest, where I slit my wrists attempting suicide. The intensity of what I was going through helped me pull up the deep emotion needed for the scene. Let me just say, as an actor, you are always typecast. I was typecast either as an intelligent, no-nonsense character or boss lady like Glenn Close; a petite slightly Southern girl like Holly Hunter; or a role with some Lucille Ball–type comedy.

Back to *Fatal Attraction*. I could not hear my acting partner. I was sitting in class when I realized that my face had also become paralyzed—Houston, we have a problem! I am an actor using my face to show emotion. People make fun of actors who Botox. Well, try having a paralyzed face where your right eye is drooping and watering constantly and your vision is blurry along with the right side of your mouth slobbering with no motor control. I could not bite, chew, or eat properly.

I don't remember my scene partner's name, but he was a cold international dude with a real hatred of women and not one ounce of emotion. Yes, acting was the perfect career choice for him. He made our rehearsals total hell.

Here's the thing. I didn't have major symptoms—no splitting headaches, no head rotations or anything like that. I did feel that something was off. I did feel like things were moving in my head. I had some dizziness and vertigo. I felt like I was an airhead—don't even say it! That tumor had to have been growing inside my head for a few years considering how large it was. If I am honest with myself, the symptoms began around 1999. Listen, I didn't want to visit negative world and stay there. I didn't want to believe something was wrong with me. You don't walk around expecting to find a tumor in your head.

Frankly, I am not a big fan of traditional doctors. For over twenty years, I had been working with holistic practitioners and energy workers and had an intense spiritual practice. Maybe these symptoms were a visit from an angel or an alien from another planet. Maybe they came to teach me something.

A few doctors I saw before said I had TMJ, temporomandibular joint syndrome, because my jaw was not opening and closing evenly or easily. In fact, any doctor who had chosen to actually look at my face and pay any attention would have seen a growth on the side of my head that in all likelihood was not original equipment.

I was trying to keep it together as all this was happening. My friend Anne from acting class was aware of what was going on with me and my health, and she said, "Don't be an idiot; don't do all of that stupid holistic stuff. My aunt died from breast cancer that way. You need to see a real doctor."

After the tough love from Anne, I decided that I did indeed need to see a medical doctor. I chose a woman because I felt like a woman might take the time to look at my face, listen, and be compassionate. Dr. Karen was a short, stocky woman with red hair and a no-nonsense manner. I said to her, "My spiritual practice is intense; what is going on with my body?" I give her credit because she didn't make fun of me. Who knew what her spiritual beliefs were, if any? She said to me in a clear, serious manner, "You need an MRI immediately." This was an effective and compassionate way to speak with me at the time.

I was shaken to find that I had a fist-sized tumor lodged in the right side of my head.

So the very next morning, I found myself at Saint Joseph Medical Center in Burbank, California, awaiting an MRI.

I was shaken to find that I had a fist-sized tumor lodged in the right side of my head. Well, holy crap; that sure explained a lot! The feeling of having a head full of too much air (again—don't you say a word), vertigo, a lack of balance, not to mention that my mouth and right eye were sagging and most of my face paralyzed. It all started to make sense then. I began to cry and then stopped myself, for I have never been a good crier. I picked myself back up and began to make some important phone calls.

Now, I take care of my health like I run my business. I take action—there's no messing around. TCB (takin' care of business) as Elvis called it. I called my husband, who was on one of his weekly business trips. I called a few friends and said, "I don't know whether you believe in prayer, but even if you don't please pray anyway. I am in trouble and need your help."

My no-nonsense Dr. Karen referred me to an otolaryngologist (an ear, nose, and throat specialist) in Glendale, which is right next door to Burbank. I could go on for pages about Dr. Glendale's office, but let me just say it was one of the worst I have ever experienced. All the nightmares were present, from incompetent office staff to nurses who treated the doctor as if he were god himself, to a huge, looming audiologist who insisted on continuing to test my left ear despite the fact that I told her it was my right ear. This misogynistic doctor had a very heavy accent and a disdainful tone of voice. The final straw was the fact that my husband was with me for support and the doctor spoke to my husband the entire time as if I weren't even there.

After leaving this chaotic office, in my heart I knew I could not tolerate a doctor who thought he was god. I needed a doctor who at a minimum would acknowledge that there is something bigger than himself. You can name this presence energy, source, God, Goddess, Buddha, Allah, Jesus, the Big Kahuna, or the great lotus flower in the sky. I was determined to find a doctor with compassion and a pleasant bedside manner, so I fired Dr. Glendale god immediately.

My next stop was the House Ear Clinic in Los Angeles. I could breathe a sigh of relief, for the communication and care were noticeably different. A biopsy was ordered, as well as a CT scan, an MRI, and a chest X-ray. I intuitively knew that the tumor was not cancerous, but the doctors insisted on a biopsy anyway.

I had become very familiar with this clinical approach from working as a standardized patient at Johns Hopkins in Baltimore, Maryland, and at UC Irvine, California. As part of teaching diplomacy and communication skills, these medical schools hired actors to portray patients. For example, I played a woman patient with cancer and had to be told that there was nothing else they could do. The cocky male medical student entered the room and announced triumphantly, "We have exhausted all possibilities, and there is nothing else we can do for you. You will live for a couple of months at the most." What? One of the reasons I trusted Dr. Slattery (you will meet him shortly) was because he never pronounced a death sentence over me. He did not predict, and he did not judge.

I decided not to become a medical doctor for a number of reasons, choosing instead to study energy medicine and intuition, and I completed a PhD in holistic psychology. I wanted to understand the 360° version of performance and also high achievers. The physical, emotional, mental, energetic, and spiritual all mattered to me.

My savior was Dr. William H. Slattery III at the House Ear Clinic. With a name like that, you'd think he was another ego doctor, but he was compassionate. Dr. Slattery performed the biopsy, and the test results came back as a rare bone tumor called a chondroblastoma. He said this type of tumor was usually found in the hip bones of young men and was very rare. I joked, "Well, I would only choose a very rare and dramatic tumor. What else could be worthy of all this time and attention?"

Why was Dr. Slattery a great communicator? Because he spoke clearly, slowly, and deliberately. He actively listened, had a serious personality, but he would laugh at my jokes. He spoke to me as if he were speaking with a colleague, respectfully. Dr. Slattery also said that he would only do the surgery if he could operate in tandem with a colleague from Cedars-Sinai Medical Center who had removed the tumor from Elizabeth Taylor's brain. I said dramatically, "Well, if it's good enough for Liz, it's good enough for me!"

By the way, if you saw the film *A Star Is Born* with Lady Gaga and Bradley Cooper, then you saw Dr. Slattery playing himself as an ear doctor.

During all this, I began to visualize a successful surgery. I ate organic foods and drank tons of filtered water. I walked daily and prayed for guidance. I picked out music that I wanted played in the operating room. Dr. Slattery preferred classic rock, and I wanted one happy surgeon in my head. If I remember correctly, music by the Eagles and the Rolling Stones was played. I also asked the medical team to refrain from saying anything that was not healing or positive while I was under anesthesia, for this is the most suggestable state a human will ever be in.

Right about now might be a good time for you to take a deep breath. The surgery went well. I was on the operating table for almost ten hours while they unraveled that tricky, sticky bone tumor from my head and facial nerve! The bones in my right ear had literally been consumed by the tumor, so the doctors sealed my right ear canal. They packed my head with fat from my lower belly (that could really come in handy for getting rid of belly fat except it was only from one side).

I was in the intensive care unit for several days, and I could not even get up to pee. Not because of the turban on my head or the twin braids (allowing fluids to drain) coming from the right side of my head. But because there was a new pain now coming from my lower belly.

It's a good thing they keep you dazed and confused so that your body is not thrown into a state of shock after the anesthesia and pain meds wear off. Not to mention, you see how bad you look, but you don't care because you are *alive*! The good-looking, kind male nurse from Kentucky (yep, there was a nurses' strike going on in LA) was kind and strong and would rotate my body because I sure as hell couldn't lift myself or turn.

The wounds did not heal, and let's just say that I wish I had purchased stock in bandages. Six months later, on April 15, 2003, I was back in the hospital because I had an infection caused by the first surgery. After that, I could finally go home and begin to heal. I had just enough energy to shower or walk or make a couple of calls each day. Sleep was precious. Dr. Slattery's orders were not to make any fast moves and not bend from the waist or lean over.

Here is one of the most puzzling things of all: afterward, no doctors came and talked to me about how I'd healed so fast or how I'd restored my health. I offered to be a counselor for others going into surgery with a tumor like mine and left my contact information with the House Ear Clinic staff. No one called. Ever. I know that these are conversations that matter and should be included in research.

If you can imagine any illness or trauma that has ever happened since life began, you can also find a person who has healed from that very thing. That is the person I would track down to the ends of the earth and ask what they did and what they learned. Would you ask a person who never had a tumor in their head what it's like? That makes absolutely no sense, but that's what I saw people doing.

Now, why practice compassion? Because you will have more positive influence when people like you and want to follow your lead. People will cooperate better. You will be aware of the fragility and preciousness of life and that folks, including you, are vulnerable. You will feel more connected to others in contrast with the frequent isolation and loneliness of running a company. And this all begins with you having compassion for yourself. Yes, it begins with you.

Let's say you are preparing a presentation to five hundred potential clients. How does all this apply to you? Because you learn to tell your story and speak with clarity by saying what matters. You learn to get to the heart of the matter and stop speaking aloud the inner dialogue going on in your head. Why does this matter? Because this way of speaking comes across as static and lacking cohesion, making it hard for us to follow you.

I learned so much about the art of truthful and compassionate communication during my illness. Part of my fast healing was because Dr. Slattery admitted that doctors don't know much about the type of tumor I had. I trusted him because he was willing to share this. His manner and speech were consistently calm and reassuring. Now, you also want your brain surgeon to be supremely confident. A friend of mine, Cathy, is a therapist who works with neurosurgeons, and she said, "You want them exhibiting some arrogance, because they cannot handle death and losing a patient." I also felt safe going into surgery because of the discussions that Dr. Slattery and I had about what the surgery would be like. Just like any life-changing event that you face, you *plan* for a positive outcome.

This is the first chapter in my book, and it is potentially the most advanced because it talks about compassion and being considerate of other people's feelings. This chapter *seems* to be about illness and death. However, if you can master the compassion lesson, your conversations will transform and the next chapters on communication will be easier.

Here in the United States, we are pretty uncomfortable and not well skilled talking about illness, trauma, or death. I was absolutely shocked and wounded at some of the things people said to me when I was going through this incredibly painful time in my life. The lack of compassion was stunning to me, and I couldn't believe some of the things I heard.

Here are some of the big offenders with a suggested reply that will offer you some emotional protection. I wish I had spoken up in a clear and strong way at the time. It would have defused my anger, and I would have taken care of myself emotionally.

∽ Is it cancer? No? Then it will be alright.

So cancer is that big bad, nasty death sentence, but a large benign tumor really is nothing at all?

∽ It's not cancer, so what is the big deal?

A tumor the size of a human fist lodged in the side of my head and rapidly creeping into my brain lining—that's the big deal.

∽ I understand.

No, you don't.

∽ You must have been a horrible person in a past lifetime; you are now paying the price.

Thanks for sharing. That's a really deep thought (you must add a very sarcastic tone to your voice for this one).

∽ This is karma for past bad things that you did.

What a compassionate and wise thing to say (again, a touch of sarcasm must be used).

∽ You only hear from one ear, so now you're handicapped.

There is nothing handicapped about me.

Some of you have faced illness or trauma, and well-meaning folks have said things to you. Forgive them for they know not and forgive yourself if you did not speak up. Let me teach you a new language—the language of communicating with compassion, sensitivity, and grace.

People have a right to every feeling even if it is uncomfortable or sad for them. That emotion is bringing them an important message. What a person is feeling is what they are feeling. I don't like when feelings are labeled positive or negative. Who gets to decide what is positive and what is negative?

Here are my top rules for communicating with compassion:

- My number one rule is don't ever say you *understand*. You don't, and you never will.

- One way to express compassion is simply to say, "I don't know what to say. Is there something I can do to help you feel better?" One of my friends in Los Angeles asked and brought me a piece of decadent chocolate cake from my favorite bakery.

- You could also say the following to someone who is facing their own mortality or a loved one's decline, "I wish I knew what to say right now, but I just don't."

- Please do not minimize or diminish our experience. It is not your job to fix us, think you can do better, or tell us what we should be feeling.

- People seem to think that c-a-n-c-e-r is a death sentence. I was dismayed to find that 99 percent of people asked me whether it was cancer. Instead, ask a person, "How do you feel about this?"

༆ The tumor in my head was my reality at the time, and I was facing it head on (pun intended). Acting like it didn't matter or asking *why me* or feeling sorry for myself were not my choices because how would that help? Don't dare suggest to someone that they are feeling sorry for themselves.

༆ Be mindful of ever calling anyone handicapped or disabled. Folks have different abilities and ways of learning, but no person should be pronounced disabled. They may have been injured and now have different abilities because of it. Let's not label folks based on what we think. If someone calls themselves blind or deaf, then you may use the same word. Listen for clues. When you are unsure, ask.

༆ Here's another suggestion while in conversation: I have never been in the hospital before, is the food really as bad as they say? When in doubt, ask gentle and thoughtful questions and then listen. I was keenly aware of how uncomfortable people were around me at the time. People would literally back away from me as if I were a monster. In fact, nearly every one of my "friends" rapidly disappeared instead of risking a deep conversation about illness and mortality.

༆ Don't share stories of how your cousin died or tell us we really should do more research or give us all kinds of helpful suggestions. If you do have a great resource, ask if it would be helpful to share. During this time people are so overloaded with fear and worry and so much information that they can't take on even one more piece of knowledge.

Now it's your turn. I have shined the light on compassionate conversations. All compassion begins with self-compassion, and with self-compassion solidly in place, we can then feel it toward others.

Think of that vulnerable person in front of you who probably holds the same dreams that you do, and promise yourself that you will do better in your conversations with others around sickness, sensitive topics, and death.

Three Ways to UpLevel Your Communication with Compassion

1. If you're a boss—practice compassion. Do you take the time to know your employees on a personal level and understand that they are not transactions but essential to your company? At a minimum find out when their birthday, anniversary, or major positive life event is and then acknowledge them on that day. There are plenty of programs and apps that can trigger reminders. You, the boss, can personally sign a card and have it delivered to their desk or home.

2. Speaking of respectful, inclusive language—the other part of successful communication is listening! Stop interrupting people, and listen without focusing on what *you* are going to say next. The very best listeners in the world are also seen as confident and successful.

   Even trees listen; modern science tells us that one of the greatest recording devices in the world is wood! Scientists have been able to extract voices and various sounds from trees. Trees record the sound of birds singing and roosting in the limbs.

3. Be vulnerable. It is only immature executives that yell at people or make demands. Does it really make any sense to yell across the office or have a temper tantrum over Zoom? Provide training to your people, give them appropriate authority, and allow them to excel. Exhibiting vulnerability reflects your humanity, confidence, and true power and will bring you loyalty.

Command Your Stage

Speak well, my friends.

Why even command your stage? Because, my friends, it's worth it! As we move into an era of more evolved and thoughtful ways of communicating, what if every conversation you had made a difference? What if you could learn to be in stillness and centered and excited all at the same time?

Think back to a time when you met someone who made a strong impression on you. A celebrity, a senator, or someone who impressed you—but you didn't recognize them at first.

I'm going to tell you a story. There I was standing in line to board a United flight to Chicago. As a frequent flyer, I had been upgraded to first class. (Happy dance! Who remembers more leg room and better service and food?) Along comes a beautifully dressed, elegant, and handsome gentleman being escorted to the front of the line by Global Services. Folks behind me began to whisper. I didn't recognize him. Chicago recognized him. It turns out this man was Christopher Gardner, the man whose life story became *The Pursuit of Happyness*, starring Will Smith. Guess who had the seat next to him?

Yours truly, and let's not talk about the Law of Attraction. He was eloquent, humble, and polite, and I began to see why his book was worthy of becoming a movie. It is positively thrilling to share meaningful conversations with those who have learned to communicate in extraordinary ways. He has learned to command his own stage.

Mr. Gardner, if you are out there reading this, I am just sure my address was lost when your suit was sent to the dry cleaner. I'd still love to receive my autographed copy of *The Pursuit of Happyness*!

Personally, I learned so much about communicating with compassion through acting. Acting also taught me how to communicate well by learning to command any stage I desired to be on.

One of my favorite clients at my consulting practice, let's call her Janice, is an executive at a well-known company in the San Francisco Bay Area. She was Russian born, French educated, in her thirties, and moving up the career ladder. She came to me because she was doing her first presentation in front of the entire company. Her talk was about tools that her colleagues could use for greater ease and efficiency. She was intelligent and accomplished but lived mostly in her rational left brain. Her delivery was stiff and uneasy, with her focus on her data instead of bringing her talk to life. She was also extremely uncomfortable with small talk in professional settings and embarrassed to show any heart or vulnerability.

I taught Janice the art of pacing her speech, inserting dramatic pauses, and generally having fun with company-wide presentations. As a result of finding her voice, she earned the respect of her colleagues and even left an unhappy marriage.

My first year in Silicon Valley, I had a client for one day who was a CFO. He worked for a woman-owned engineering firm in Palo Alto, California. Michael told me that he only presented to other CFOs. I was coaching him because the company he worked for was winning an award and that meant he was going to be on a different stage. The audience was different. Michael refused to smile because he said all CFOs are serious and do not smile. I believe he was selling himself and other CFOs short. Maybe CFOs do not smile because no one has ever commanded the stage and told them a funny story. There is absolutely no reason money, projections, and budgets cannot be made into a fun and provocative talk. Michael was an uptight engineering type who was prone to mansplaining and lecturing. My uncompliant client would not budge one inch. He refused to smile. This was unlike Janice, who was a happier person because of her newfound confidence in presenting. She transformed her life through learning. I didn't get to witness Michael's acceptance speech, but I can only imagine it was forgettable.

Throughout this chapter and my book, I'm going to refer to "showing heart" or "opening your heart." What I mean by "opening your heart" is allowing your humanity to show. These are the traits of tenderness, compassion, empathy, and understanding. Be vulnerable. The heart has tremendous power and intelligence and when combined with the intelligence of your mind, is unstoppable. A boss that is truly admired demonstrates their passion by showing their heart. If you are focused on impressing us with only your brain, you will not reach all the audience. People want to know that you care about them and their contribution.

Let's go back to the basics. What do I mean by *stage*? The definition of the word *stage* is multifold. It can range from a step in a process, to a raised platform,

Your stage is wherever you are standing.

to a place suitable for presentation. The origin of the word is a Latin term meaning *to stand*. So your stage is wherever you are standing. It could be an auditorium, a boardroom, a pulpit, a dais, a position in front of a video camera, or even a street in the city. It could also include your bedroom, but that's a whole other book. I invite you to think of your stage as being both where you are standing and being suitable for *your* presentation.

And what does *command* even mean? Some of the clients in my consulting business tell me that the word intimidates them a little. And it certainly does sound a bit aggressive, maybe bringing to mind the thought of military officers commanding other people.

It's fascinating to pull language apart and see how words were born. Some words have changed remarkably from their original context and meaning.

Take the word *command*. Most people think of its meaning as "to order" or "to compel." Compel means "to drive," especially to a course of action. Compel also means to have a powerful and irresistible effect. And, if we delve even deeper, command also means "expertise" or "mastery." Rolling back all the way to the thirteenth-century origin of command, it means to "entrust" or "enjoin." So now you know where I am coming from, and let me be quite clear that when I talk about *commanding a stage*, I am not talking about barking orders or being that boss who thinks the only way to communicate is to yell.

In fact, this is exactly what happened to me last week when I was dining at a popular place featuring upscale hot dogs and craft beer. The owner, clearly an alpha dog, began to loudly bark orders from the moment my husband and I entered the line. "Stand on the yellow line out of the way. Leave the exit clear." He then yelled in my direction, "Use the men's room; don't wait for the women's room to be free." If I'm going to be given orders the minute I enter an establishment, I will need to see a warning printed on the menu. This was not *commanding a stage* (which, in his case, was his restaurant).

To truly command his stage would have meant to warmly welcome customers in, capably manage his staff, and behave as if he were the conductor of a beautifully run restaurant that we wanted to return to.

UpLevel Your Communication goes beyond simply being a book on giving presentations. Over the next eight chapters detailing my ten-plus years of coaching high-performing leaders, I will be revealing my insider tips for delivering a presentation that really helps you shine.

There are three essential parts to commanding your stage:

1. Prestage

2. The speech itself

3. Closing / the wrap-up

The most important time will always be your time on the stage itself.

Before agreeing to speak or present and before you ever sit down to begin writing your outline, there are some important questions you need to ask yourself.

Here are some questions that you can ask:

- What type of speech is this—a keynote, for a company? Is it a panel, for an organization, etc.?

- Who is my audience?

- What is the size of my audience?

- What is the size and feel of the stage?

- Is my stage live or virtual, and what is the platform?

- What will the dynamics and breakdown be—is the audience men, women, people who identify otherwise?

- What is the age range?

- What is the education level, and is it narrow or broad?

- Do I have people from all over the world or a more local crowd?

- If I speak with a religious group or other specific group, what language do I want to use or avoid?

- What is the purpose of my talk?

- Why me? Why was I the one asked to speak?

- How long do I have to speak?

- Who will introduce me, and how will I be introduced?

- Will I be answering questions?

- Do I have a call to action?

- What do I want my audience to take away?

- How do I want my audience to feel?

You might think all those questions sound good, but the ultimate question ... bugle call ... is *why* are you speaking? Identify three or four reasons (from the following list) right from the beginning. I promise this will change the way you put together your speech and also the way you deliver it.

Here are some possible reasons, intentions, or qualities that you want to bring to or embody with your talk:

- Educate or teach

- Enlighten

- Challenge

- Motivate

- Get elected to an office or a position

- ↩ Sell

- ↩ Give instructions

- ↩ Influence

- ↩ Fundraise for a worthy cause

- ↩ Secure funds for your company

- ↩ Alienate (OK, I put that in here for dramatic purposes but also because I have seen presentations that did just this.)

Once you gather the demographics, psychographics, and your big why, you can begin the outline of your presentation. I like to outline my talking points—three or four at most for forty-five minutes to an hour of presenting. First, I decide my nonnegotiables. Those are the things that I must absolutely, positively say even if all he** breaks loose. When the mic goes down, the power goes out, and your time is cut to fifteen minutes, these are the crucial parts of your speech. When I first began to speak in public, I didn't know any of this and didn't have a solid structure for my talks. The show must go on, and if you have committed these three or four things to heart with practice, you will remember the core of your talk. Always rehearse and rehearse because things will happen, but you can still pull off your talk with confidence!

Listening to a great presentation is going to take me on a roller coaster ride. It is going to make me think and make me feel and give me a glimpse inside your world that only you can share. One of your jobs in commanding the stage is to pull back the Oz curtain. This is never about reciting a PowerPoint; this is about bringing your material to life. This is all about your delivery. By that I mean it's your tone of voice, it's the way you stand, it's the way you tell a story, it's the words you choose, it's your passion, and it's the way you inspire the audience to care. You are the way-shower—so take us somewhere wonderful.

One way to write your presentation is to structure it in what I call a rainbow arc—it starts down near the ground on the left and then takes us to the high point in the middle and then delivers us happily back on the ground to the right. All of us want to find the pot of gold at the end of the rainbow. Plan your segments and your timing. Always end on time or a couple minutes before. Leave 'em wantin' more!

Now, let's turn the page and get back to *your* time on stage.

The key element that every great speaker knows is how to stay in their body, thinking clearly. What I mean by that is they don't become a talking head or a PowerPoint reader. They take ownership of their content, delivery, and energy; and as a result, they command the stage, their stage.

This is also a person who practices and prepares in order to be more comfortable and do a great job. Speakers who do TED Talks prepare for at least six months up to one year before they are filmed. And there is a reason why we rehearse for weeks and weeks before opening night in the theater.

First, here are three effective techniques to master your fears and calm your nervous system:

1. Understand that your body does not know the difference between fear and excitement, so select excitement.

2. Feeling nervous simply means that you care, remember that!

3. Walking fast while swinging your arms, dancing, and gently shaking your whole body are great ways to warm up and get the energy flowing more evenly throughout your body before you speak.

Second, try these techniques to calm your nerves and keep blood and oxygen going to your core and brain instead of your extremities. These practices help you stay in your body and not turn into the dreaded "talking head executive":

- Count backward slowly from ten to one, breathing through your nose in between each number.

- Meditate, pray, or chant.

- Focus your thoughts in your heart space, and imagine your heart is open to connect to others. The energy from your heart carries much further than the energy from your brain. In fact, your heart sends more messages to your brain than your brain sends to your heart. So where is the true intelligence?

- Craft a custom affirmation to repeat to yourself. I have suggested a few here:

    - "I have something important to say, and people want to hear me."

    - "When I speak, I change lives."

    - "This is not about me; this is about my audience."

    - "My voice matters, and I choose to make a difference."

    - "The world is my stage, and I'm here!"

Third, take up more space on the stage. Did you ever listen to a speaker who seemed to be apologizing for being on stage or for taking up space? An executive who does not appear to be confident will not be influential and impactful from stage.

A person who is pulling in their energy is unconsciously limiting themselves. Your posture should be tall, and you should come across as someone worth listening to.

During my undergrad days, my degree program was music business with a voice minor. My singing teacher was German and had escaped Nazi Germany during World War II and came to the United States for freedom. She would say to me, "You need to take up more space when singing opera." It took me years to understand what she really meant by that statement. Opera is an intense art form that requires superhuman stamina along with command of your voice and body!

Here's how you take up more space:

- Physically stand tall with your chest lifted and your ribs wide and expanded.

- Stand with your feet parallel and even while feeling rooted or anchored into Mother Earth.

- Imagine shooting your energy to the moon and back.

- Now imagine sending your energy to each of the four corners at the ceiling and four corners at the floor, expanding your energy and making it stronger.

Have you ever noticed a sign language interpreter on stage? The great ones know they are not the center of attention. But as they sign, some move and dance and they bring the beauty of the language to life. This is a great example of someone who is commanding the stage in the very best way.

Fourth, your voice must have a rich quality or resonance that gives it carrying power from the stage. There's a bit more that I must share with you about the voice, as many people take it for granted because they can speak.

To me, the voice is the first instrument—it begins with your birth cry! With your voice, you can communicate feelings, tell a story, give instructions, imitate, encourage change, make an impact, ask me to repeat after you, pitch a product, or hurt me. The voice can be healing or can be used as a weapon of destruction with cruelty and belittling.

- ✎ Your voice has a destination point, and that is the back row or the back wall.

- ✎ A healthy voice is produced with even air flow while feeling the air and sound are coming up and out of your throat.

- ✎ Most people speak too fast. Choose a pace or speed so that all can hear and understand your words.

- ✎ Know that the art of the pause is one of the most effective tools you can use.

- ✎ Practice your enunciation as well as the correct pronunciation of each word, including each person's name, out loud.

Fifth, remember the audience is out there and you want to reach them. This applies to a huge auditorium as well as a Zoom video chat with clients.

- ✎ Your eyes need to work the room in a large space. You will begin in the center and then look left or look right, always making sure to continue to move your gaze to everyone in the room.

- ✎ You want to be aware of facing out and maintaining 75 percent of your body forward. If you are pointing to a slide or need to draw attention to something, you will pivot your body slightly. In show business, we call this "cheating out," so that you never turn your back on the audience.

Sixth, plan your wrap-up, close, or invitation carefully. I have observed folks who are going to do what we call "sell from the stage" and something shifts dramatically when they move into the sales conversation. I have witnessed people who literally sounded like a different person. You will never make those sales if you don't develop confidence and keep your message clear to the end. Plan your speech all the way to the applause!

- Practice your transition into closing or selling or the call to action (buy my book!).

- Maintain your energy, voice quality, and strong body posture.

- If you are going to take questions, plan for this and practice how you will respond.

- End on time. Really. Businesspeople who are great speakers honor their commitment and show respect by ending on time or even slightly before.

Three Ways to UpLevel Your Communication by Commanding Your Stage

1. Take up more space. Literally. Stand tall. Don't ever apologize for being on a stage. Take ownership of your presentation, and decide that you will command any stage that you are privileged to be invited on.

Don't ever apologize for being on a stage.

2. Stay in your body. Your whole body. Do not allow your energy to creep up so that you live in your head. Stay involved.

3. Open your heart, and realize that you will never truly connect with your audience unless you allow vulnerability. Sensitivity is one of your greatest strengths as a leader. Sensitivity is not a female or male thing; it is a human thing.

It's your turn. Review all the insider secrets and techniques that I revealed in this chapter, test them to find out your favorites, and then create your very own command-the-stage ritual.

Next up, we dive deep into the world of vocal archetypes, something I created based on the phases of a person's life. My clients have found that a custom "vocal recipe" creates an understanding of how and when to use their voice because our voice is not a tangible thing that we can see. Join me!

My Vocal Archetypes^{SM} System

Archetypes reveal patterns of self-knowledge for our success.

For most of my life, I have studied religion, spirituality, and metaphysics. I have found that each and every religion or practice has a beauty, a code of morality, and a guide to suggested behaviors. One of my most meaningful discoveries was Goddess spirituality. This was where I found my center, my home. This form of consciousness showed respect for women unlike any other church or temple I had ever been to. A woman who did marketing for the holistic, spiritual crowd told me about the temple at a business meeting in Burbank. I don't remember what we were talking about, but she said, "Are you aware that there is a Goddess Temple in Orange County?" "Excuse me," I said, "a what?"

Many people think Los Angeles is packed with conscious, Goddess people, but that's not actually the case. Orange County, in particular, has a reputation for its wealthy, conservative Christian population. I am a curious type, always seeking to discover, so you know that I had to find out for myself. Very early one Sunday morning, I headed off for a two-hour drive south to Irvine, California. I arrived at a nondescript industrial park next door to John Wayne Airport. The main room was small, beautifully decorated, a sanctuary of beautifully dressed women filling all the chairs and sitting on pillows on the floor. There were candles and incense, flowers, and statues of Sekhmet, Isis, Oshun, Quan Yin, and Aphrodite … it was strange, and it was wonderful. I had no idea what to do and hoped that I did not make any embarrassing mistakes. I experienced the ritual, and I admit I was uncomfortable, intrigued, and comforted all at the same time.

Goddess culture means that everything is sacred, we are all connected, and that all forms of life are to be honored, including all peoples, animals, and Mother Earth. Women are to be honored and respected because we are the givers of life. The birthers of children, beauty, intuition, and spiritual wisdom are not second-class citizens. The Goddess is known by many names and represents each and every aspect of woman. She is big enough to hold all religions and does not discriminate.

There are many forms of Goddess spirituality and many books written. Some of the most interesting and enlightening authors to me are *Jean Houston, Max Dashu, Rev. Dr. Karen Tate, Heide Goettner-Abendroth, Starhawk, Ava Park, and Joseph Campbell.*

Most teachings declare that there are three phases of a woman's life. The first is the Maiden, meaning the fresh young girl who loves to sing and dance. The next phase is the Mother, meaning the nurturing woman who gives birth to babies and companies. Finally, we have the Crone, meaning the woman who has experience; she is the wise grandmother. Hold on, let's stop things right there! Using only three phases completely leaves out what could be the most productive and fulfilling phase of a woman's life—the Queen phase.

The Queen phase typically occurs around ages forty-five to around sixty-five years for a woman. What I have witnessed is that the Queen has been erased out of almost all religions, traditions, and houses because of her very power and because she cannot be so easily manipulated. The Queen in stories, literature, films, and fairy tales is depicted as evil and greedy. Just when a woman has finally mastered some confidence, wisdom, and experience, we don't want to hear from her anymore.

> **The Queen has been erased out of almost all religions, traditions, and houses because of her very power and because she cannot be so easily manipulated.**

The same applies to the phases of a man's life. The traditional three-phase model would say phase one is the Boy, meaning the wild young man. Secondly, we have the Father, meaning the man who has a family or a company and protects his children. Finally, the Grandfather, meaning the old man who has been around the block a few times. This is so limiting and boring. The three-phase model completely leaves out the King or sovereign phase for a man. Just when he finally has the knowledge and wisdom and discipline at around age fifty to run an empire, the good King is dismissed.

What can you, the executive, learn from archetypes? I don't remember when the lightbulb went off, but one day I understood that the archetypes I had studied so diligently applied to our voices!

Your physical age does not matter, as you have each archetype within you and can use any one of them at any time. Our voices have more capabilities, colors, and qualities than you have probably ever thought of. Using your imagination to enhance some of those colors and flavors will change the way you, the executive, speak a message that lands and changes the way you are perceived by others.

What all my years of study in religion and spirituality have taught me is that our voices mirror our life phases—and that each aspect of our spirit is available to be used in any way at any time. Each one of the four aspects is an archetype and can be used for self-awareness and effective communication.

So I began to create a custom recipe for each client that came to me. I pulled qualities from each archetype and introduced specific applications depending on the purpose of the communication. And what do you know? I was onto something as I tested it with each of my clients. I began to notice that these professionals started to develop a deep confidence and a shift in their voice and executive presence.

For example, the CEO of a company delivering a state-of-the-company keynote would almost exclusively use their benevolent Queen or King voice. This is the voice of the one who knows and has vision and should be managing resources well on behalf of the entire company. This is not the time to speak with the Maiden or Lad voice.

The professional who has authored a book and is reading from it would have a vocal recipe made up of the Queen or King with a touch of the wise old storyteller. The recipe when it's a children's book could be a mix of Grandma or Grandpa sharing the story with some of the Maiden or Lad voice added for vocal variety and pure fun.

Let's explore the names, qualities, and ways to use each archetype, beginning with the traditional three-aspect model and adding the (mistakenly and very important) missing sovereign fourth phase.

In this book, I will address only the archetypes for women and for men, as there are so many recipes you can cook up with just these two. You can also combine both female and male archetypes for your unique voice. Some of you don't identify with the binary of male or female, and I invite you to explore and create your own delicious recipes!

Archetypes for Women

First, we begin with the Maiden, also known as the Girl:

- Average age range: birth to about twenty

- Associations: spring and the element of air

- Actor portrayals: Shirley Temple as a little girl and Reese Witherspoon in *Legally Blonde*

- Qualities: youthfulness, fun, energy, speed, wildness, happiness, health, laughter, defiance, enthusiasm, and bossiness (like a girl demonstrating early leadership qualities)

- Tone: breathy, enthusiastic, fast-paced, spontaneous, and high-pitched

When should you use the Maiden voice?

- When going out with your girlfriends, playing with your children, teaching or working with young children, demonstrating fun or playfulness, feeling silly, or playing games—think Twister or Candy Land, not poker.

- In a professional setting, your Maiden voice could be used when speaking with very young coworkers or interns to connect more with them. It could also be used when expressing happiness, demonstrating a toy, or telling a silly (yet appropriate) joke to lighten up a heavy atmosphere.

Second, enter the Mother:

- Average age range: around twenty to forty-five

- Associations: summer and the element of fire

⌁ Actor portrayal: Marilu Henner in *Aurora Teagarden Mysteries*

⌁ Qualities: nurturing, unconditional mother's love, romantic love, passion, heat, beauty, fire, compassion, and the voice of a protector—whether gentle or fierce

⌁ Tone: loving, firm, emotional, and slower paced with children

When should you use the Mother voice?

⌁ With your kids, when passion or heat is called for, to speak with compassion, in the role of a caretaker, to speak love, or to add the quality of loveliness

⌁ In a professional setting, your Mother voice would be used when expressing compassion or empathy for a coworker or employee. It could also be used when delivering bad news, protecting someone, cooling tempers, or warming the atmosphere.

Third, we have the Crone, also known as the Grandmother, Sage, Elder, or Wisewoman:

⌁ Average age range: sixty-five and older

⌁ Associations: winter and the element of earth

⌁ Actor portrayal: Dr. Maya Angelou in *Roots*

⌁ Qualities: wisdom, experience, storytelling, earthiness, calmness, safety, and kindness

⌁ Tone: mature, measured, experienced, and healthy, and lower pitched

When should you use the Sage voice?

- When reading to children, speaking to your grandchildren, teaching the next generations, or just being you and winding down for the evening

- In a professional setting, use your Crone voice when negotiating, teaching, helping parties come to agreement, or when grounding is called for.

May I have a drumroll please? We will finish with the Queen because she is the most important for women. Now, thanks to the Dr. Miluna Fausch method and the addition of this fourth phase, you will add more strings to your bow, more colors to your palette, more range to your voice:

- Average age range: forty-five to sixty-five

- Associations: fall and the element of water

- Actor portrayal: Angela Lansbury in *Murder, She Wrote*

- Qualities: vision, knowledge, discernment for all, necessary firmness, maker and holder of boundaries, benevolence, grace, regalness, and intuition

- Tone: full breathed, rich, resonant, dynamic, commanding, unemotional, steady, rich, and sufficiently loud

When do you use the Queen voice?

- During family meetings, when expressing and asking for excellence and high standards, or when establishing boundaries with family, friends, or coworkers

∽ In a professional setting, use your Queen voice when you are the boss, leading a board meeting, pitching for funding, or asking for a raise. It could also be used when restoring order or fighting for justice in the courtroom. In an emergency, it's the only voice that will be heard when summoning help or evacuating a plane!

The voice and power of the good Queen are what keep the Maiden safe, the Mother from being completely burned out from always putting others first, and the Sage healthy and strong in later years. She is the one who speaks the truth with vision and compassion. The Queen is the one who knows where her company should go and how to lead it. She is the one who knows when to leave a bad relationship or job. She has learned to be her own woman and not a people pleaser.

The Queen has found her voice!

The Queen has *found* her voice!

In many companies flying the patriarchal flag, the Maiden voice can be ignored for her youth, the Mother voice interrupted for expressing too much emotion or vulnerability, and the Sage voice dismissed because she is considered old. The Queen and her voice are essential in business. It is the Queen who must speak up for herself, her purpose, and her vision for the company or business as a whole.

Let me tell you about a client of mine, whom we'll call Marianne. She was in middle management for a well-established company in Sunnyvale, California. Marianne was well educated, well traveled, and ambitious, and she wanted to move into the C-suite. She came to me to build a better voice. Her voice was too soft and carried too many high-pitched Maiden qualities in it. She was frequently interrupted and felt she was not heard.

Marianne needed to find her Queen voice: a voice that sounded richer and more powerful. It was there—it was just buried under the good-daughter belief system. She needed to speak in a voice that reflected her experience and skill. I began by teaching her how to introduce herself with a confident handshake and using her first and last name. Post COVID-19 we may not be shaking hands any longer. I will address introductions, eye contact, and body language in this new era in a later chapter. We worked on her posture and executive presence, as she was a petite lady surrounded by a leadership team of tall alpha males. We practiced making more eye contact and selecting a posture that said, "I can hold my own."

Marianne learned to lift her voice out of her throat and use more volume. I had her practice being loud, really loud. When you have been taught to be quiet and submissive, you must experience the sound and feeling of having volume. We worked on more brevity and clarity in her way of speaking and making her points. I also taught her the art of interrupting (more on my methods of interrupting in a later chapter), and she embraced the techniques that were most authentic to her style.

Now let's move into the archetypes for men. The same principles apply, and I won't spend too much time here, except to explain that many times the King is seen as evil or selfish just like the Queen is portrayed. It's not fair. Being a King should not suggest that a person is greedy or rich or manipulative, putting his own needs above those of his kingdom. On the other hand, don't get me started on King Henry VIII!

Archetypes for Men

First up is the Lad or the Boy:

- Average age range: birth to around twenty

- Associations: spring and the element of air

- Actor portrayal: Kevin Bacon in *Footloose*

- Qualities: youth, strength, wildness, happiness, joy, fun, disinhibition, speed, and energy

- Tone: breathy, high energy, fast-paced, wild, and perhaps higher pitched

When should you use your Lad voice?

- When playing, hanging out with your friends, being a young comedian, and expressing unabashed fun, joy, and happiness

- In a professional setting, use your Lad voice for expressing fun, working with college students or young interns, telling a (appropriate) joke, or expressing enthusiasm or support.

Second, we have the Father:

- Average age range: around twenty to forty-five

- Associations: summer and the element of fire

- Actor portrayal: Daniel Henney in *Criminal Minds*

- Qualities: devotion, strength, protection, provider, love, lover, and passion

- Tone: protective, smart, even breathed, and slower paced with children

When do you use your Father voice?

- With your children, when protecting, with your own father, or when with other dads

- In a professional setting, use your Father voice when delivering bad news, expressing compassion, being passionate about your mission, or fighting for what's right.

Coming up third is the King:

- Average age range: forty-five to sixty-five

- Associations: fall and the element of water

- Actor portrayal: Colin Firth in *The King's Speech*

- Qualities: vision, oversight of the whole realm, responsibility, trust, firmness, compassion, wisdom, and discernment

- Tone: dynamic, strong, rich and powerful, and equal parts breath and pitch

When do you use your King voice?

- As you serve others, as the leader, or when you are trying to encourage trust in yourself

- In a professional setting, use your King voice when you are the boss and when leading a board meeting. It could also be used when running for office, establishing or maintaining law and order, or getting help in an emergency.

And last but not least, we have the Elder, also known as the Grandfather or Wizard:

- Average age range: sixty-five and older

- Associations: winter and the element of earth

- Actor portrayal: Morgan Freeman in *The Bucket List*

- Qualities: wisdom, experience, storytelling, earthiness, steadiness, kindness, and understanding

- Tone: mature, steady and slower paced, and lower pitched

When do you use your Elder voice?

- As you tell stories, when reading to your grandkids, when handling situations between generations, or with your elder friends

- In a professional setting, use your Elder voice when mentoring, negotiating, expressing experience, or inviting new folks in.

There are an infinite number of recipe combinations. I want to show you two ways to put together a recipe for success using the qualities of each archetype.

Custom Recipe 1

Let's say you are an engineer who is going to make a pitch for a new widget on behalf of your division. It's a widget that is 50 percent the same as the old widget with 50 percent improved efficiency and function. You are the one who has the vision for why your company should begin to manufacture the new and improved widget. And you've got to prove it without any track record.

Your recipe would look like this:

From the Kitchen of William D. Engineer

Ingredients:

75% King voice—a rich, trusted voice with carrying power

15% Father-knows-best voice—warm and wise with openness

5% Enthusiastic Lad voice—a voice that carries the excitement and belief of a young boy

5% Elder—a voice of experience, a tone that is deliberate along with a slower pace

Begin to speak strongly with your trusted King voice as you travel through the research and explanation of the new widget. Add some vocal variety on the data and numbers with your Father-knows-best voice. As you demonstrate the 3-D widget to the audience, add 5 percent fun discovery with your Lad voice. As you wrap up, move into your Elder, the voice of experience to convince us of the success you know is possible.

Custom Recipe 2

For this recipe, let's say you are a woman interviewing for a board seat. Picture yourself sitting in a power seat for visibility. The power seat is one where the CEO, board president, influencer, or the leader of the meeting can clearly see and hear you. When you enter the room, you must assess where the power seats are going to be. This is something that I teach my clients, and I will address this more in the context of the current state of business and virtual meetings in later chapters. But for the purposes of this recipe, let's say you have worked for years across three industries to gather experience and credibility. You climbed that so-called career ladder to success. Your résumé is skillfully written and up to date. Your professional clothing is ready and flattering; we women are still judged much more than men on what we are wearing and how we look.

Your recipe would look like this:

From the Kitchen of Faith N. Board

Ingredients:

70% Queen voice—a full, strong voice that demonstrates your leadership superpowers

20% Sage voice—you speak with a tone that is deliberate and rich with experience

10% Maiden voice—a voice that demonstrates your youthful energy to get the job done. Do *not* speak in a higher pitch!

Begin with a combination of your solid, benevolent Queen voice with some Maiden added when you smile and say your name. As you share your vast talent and experience, talk with your Queen and your Sage voices. Let the Sage speak when you relate case studies or results that led to the growth of your company. When you tell a funny story or bring up a blooper, use that Maiden voice full of fun and enthusiasm.

Do you see how putting together a recipe gives you vocal variety and range and adds interest and influence to your voice and verbal communication? And it's fun for you and your audience.

People want to assign meaning and believe in confident leaders with heart. Dance that changemaker dance, and show the way!

Three Ways to UpLevel Your Communication Using Vocal Archetypes

1. Begin to change your thinking about what is possible. What qualities do you want to convey with your voice and energy? I recommend that you start thinking of your voice and desired archetype recipes in the shower, where some of our greatest ideas happen!

2. Study the qualities and applications of each vocal archetype. Think of your company or business, and jot down your current goals. When could you use each archetype for better results? For more influence? To increase sales?

   I have found in my practice that I literally coach executives on when to vary their voices. It takes practice to figure out where the vocal shifts need to be.

3. You must practice out loud with your voice. Remember, your voice is a *physical* thing. Do it when you are alone so that you are not self-conscious and holding back. You will be amazed at how much more influential and effective you are when you have mastery over your spoken communication.

Now that you have discovered and delved into my Vocal Archetypes℠ system for women and men, we are going to enter the delicious world of beautiful and inclusive language in chapter 4.

What do I mean by beautiful and inclusive language? Well, it means choosing words that uplift another rather than tear them down. It means language that causes us to sit up taller and listen better because we are not hearing the usual clichés and tired phrases. It means not making up ridiculous words, acronyms, or phrases that are designed to impress but just confuse. And it means doing your very best to address everyone in the room, not just people who look and act like you.

CHAPTER 4

Beautiful and Inclusive Language

Every language in the world has a word for thank you.

The idea for this chapter was partially birthed from a personal conversation that I had. I was on a three-way call with two other people and was considering forming a partnership with them. The second person in our trio was a neuro-linguistic programmer and energy practitioner whom we'll call Crystal. The third person on the call was a Greek man who billed himself as a start-up expert and thought leader lifting up humanity. We'll call him Aristotle. The three of us would potentially form an alliance and teach from our field of expertise in universities throughout the world. I don't remember how our conversation started, but Crystal said something like "I don't care what I say anymore; I just need to tell it like it is." Sure enough, a few minutes later, she did. She accused me of not contributing because my phone did not have certain features activated. Crystal aggressively said to me that "I needed to get with it, get with the program."

Well, let me tell you that pushed just about every button on me. Remember that I was under the impression that they were both compassionate, evolved spiritual beings. In fact, Crystal and I had had a couple of talks in which I believed that we had connected sister to sister. Clearly, I was wrong. I told her that her tone and words were hurtful to me. She replied, "You took it all wrong." I could feel my heart ache and my throat close. I literally could not speak. How was it OK to shut down other people in a conversation? And to make things even more painful, uplift-humanity-man Aristotle joined with her.

Well, saying "you took it all wrong" is immature. Because when we "tell it like it is," that is a monologue—it's a solo act. It is our perspective, which may not leave room for any other perspective. Don't get me wrong. I will say there *are* times to "tell it like it is." For instance, this includes when there is danger, theft, or abuse. I have completed a few self-defense classes. If you are a woman in danger of being attacked, you do not yell *rape* you yell the word *stop*. If you had to assist in evacuating a plane you would strongly say, "Get off the plane." There is also another circumstance in which "tell it like it is" does apply. Comedy. Good comedy works because it is shocking and real and plays with speech. You don't want comedians mincing their words. Comedians break all my rules of polite communication! Imagine if Joan Rivers had been polite and gentle—it would not have worked.

But when you are unhappy with the way someone did or did not do something, there are much better ways to respond. Going back to that three-way call, I decided that Crystal's communication skills were aggressive and insensitive. It struck me that this wasn't the first time that Crystal had spoken to me in a strident, unfriendly way. My personal belief was that she had unresolved issues with other women, and I let the relationship go. The bottom line was that her manner of communication made me feel like I just didn't matter.

In this chapter, I am *not* going to be asking you to stop expressing yourself or to lie. I am asking you to understand that the words you use and how you speak to others can be hurtful. Relationships can and do fall apart because of insensitive speaking and the need to make others feel that they are in some way wrong.

As an executive, you desire to have an influence and impact. Always bear in mind that there are words and ways of speaking that will attract people to you, not repel them. Also understand that how you deliver your words is going to reflect on how your message is received at the other end. When you are writing a speech or leading a meeting, it really helps to make a plan so that your words are thoughtful. When you think of thought leaders whom you admire, they are more than likely skilled at communication. They have learned how to get their message out so that it's heard. Personally, I'm drawn to folks like Maya Angelou, reading a passage from "Still I Rise" in her rich honey voice. And I love hearing the magnetic voice of Simon Sinek sharing from his book *Start with Why* on a TED Talk.

As the world grows smaller, we need to understand that we are interacting with people from all over the world and that we are all connected. I invite you to get out of "comfortable world" and expand your sense of community. I love the butterfly effect story, which suggests that the flap of a butterfly's wings in one country could cause a tornado in another. Every word we speak or action we take has an effect on someone else. People who come to the United States usually speak a language other than English. They come from a different culture, and their professionalism may look different. Think of it this way: if you want to be a great world traveler, you study the culture before you travel to another country. Perhaps you learn a few words like *please, thank you,* and *you're welcome.* For instance, *thank you* in Spanish is *gracias. Thank you* in French is *merci. Thank you* in Swiss German is *danke schön* in the formal or *danke* in the informal. There are different nuances in other languages that English does not have. I know from my own experience that demonstrating respect and courtesy can take you around the world with ease. While you might feel embarrassed by your lack of vocabulary in another language, people tend to be delighted by the fact that you learned basic words of courtesy. If you allow yourself to be vulnerable in speaking another language and watch the effect that your words are having on others, your understanding of speech will be richer.

Ah, the chances of being misunderstood are high. Very high. And there is another reason to use what I call "smart, heart communication." It's because of the high cost of miscommunication. Smart, heart communication is one of my "Miluna-isms," and it means honest speaking from the heart. Ineffective and sloppy communication costs companies millions of dollars each year. I call this "murky talk."

A 2017 article by the World Economic Forum reported that "miscommunication costs businesses with up to 100 staff an average of US $420,000 per year. Even more staggeringly, in another study, 400 businesses with at least 100,000 employees each claimed that inadequate communication cost an average of US $62.4 million per company per year."[1]

I believe these numbers to be an underestimate, especially given how much business has changed since 2017. Now that we are not interacting face-to-face as much, we are missing visual cues, body language clues, and the touch of a handshake. Speaking with a person

---

1   Libby Sander, "In the Workplace of the Future, These Are the Skills Employers Want," World Economic Forum, March 7, 2017, https://www.weforum.org/agenda/2017/03/in-the-workplace-of-the-future-these-are-the-skills-employers-want.

on the phone can be rather impersonal, and I have found that folks will say things over the phone that they would never say to me in person.

Here's an example: one time I made a phone call about an error on a bill that happened to be around $1.29. The operator laughed and actually said to me, "What's the big deal? It's a buck!" I said to her, "The big deal is that if you make small errors, what other errors are being made?" At that point, she acknowledged that what I was saying was important and apologized to me. Had we been face-to-face, I feel that she would have been less flippant and more professional.

Let me tell you a funny story about being misunderstood. Many years back I worked as an executive assistant to a man at a professional association in Columbus, Ohio. We'll call him Jim. We could not have been more opposite. He was tall and uncoordinated. We had an open cubicle office layout, and his extremely loud speaking voice would carry the entire length of the building. Jim is the guy on the airplane who sits next to you, takes all the elbow room and leg room, and begins an 85 decibel conversation at you. He possessed absolutely zero self-awareness. He was married with children and spoke to his wife as if she were the village idiot. Yet, on paper, he had a solid résumé and background. Now because I am a relator-type personality, I kept searching for any common ground between us. One day Jim mentioned jazz. I got very excited because I thought, finally, after two years we had something to talk about. Can you guess what comes next? I was thinking jazz, as in jazz music, and he meant jazz, as in the Utah Jazz basketball team. Drat, foiled again! Here's the thing—behind Jim's back, people talked about him and his lack of emotional intelligence combined with inappropriate behavior. If he had considered feedback from the boss to develop his executive communication and presence, he could have progressed both in his career and in his personal relationships.

As an executive you cannot assume that people are thinking the same thing you are. I am asking you to speak in a respectable and honorable way so that you can lower the risk of being misunderstood. Because to you the word *jazz* means a basketball team and to me it means a genre of music.

Let's move now into what I call clear, courteous, conscious, courageous, compassionate, and 'clusive (meaning inclusive and get a clue) language arts.

And let's start with my least favorite word in the entire universe. This word makes me want to plug my ears and stick out my tongue. I am now so sensitive to it that I cringe. I can barely stand to say it but here goes: guys. *Guys* this and *guys* that. Hey, guys! What's up, guys? Well, I wouldn't know, would I, because I'm not a guy. Stop! Stop saying that word! OK, I've calmed down now. But if that didn't come through loud and clear, here are some reasons to stop using *guy* as your default word:

- *Guy* is an informal word for man or boy. The word is masculine, and it is too informal for polite company and international business.

- In British slang, a guy is a person in shabby or ludicrously odd clothes. Does this describe most people? The answer is no.

- Your audience is filled with men, women, and folks who identify otherwise.

- As a leader, your responsibility is to include everyone in the meeting, the room, or the conversation. You have a chance to evolve your language so that no one is left out or unintentionally offended.

So what do you say instead?

The number one word my clients choose is *folks*. It is warm and welcoming with a hint of Southern charm. Other inclusive phrases are, "Welcome, everyone"; "Good morning, everybody"; "Good afternoon"; "Hello, team"; "Good day, [your company's name]"; "Welcome to the meeting, all"; and "Thanks to each of you for being here today." When you are hosting a small meeting, greet everyone by name. Most everyone loves to hear their own name and to be acknowledged. The fact that you understand the importance of this marks you as a true leader.

> **When you are hosting a small meeting, greet everyone by name.**

It makes me feel special when folks take the time to ask me what I would like to be called or ask how to pronounce my name correctly. I never forget their courtesy and respect. When in doubt, simply ask a person how you should address them. And don't forget, on LinkedIn you can now record your name so that others may hear you speak in your own voice and how you would like to be addressed.

The second thing that bugs me and is worth mentioning is a commonly heard phrase. Although, I must say, I don't hear it as much as I used to. It's the phrase "no problem." When I hear that phrase, all I really hear is the word *problem*. In metaphysical teachings we are taught that the universe cancels the word *no*, which means we are left with *problem* reverberating throughout the galaxy. Don't we have enough problems in the world without speaking more into existence?

So what do you say instead?

Well, you can respond with "You're welcome," "Of course," or "My pleasure." At some of the best hotels in the world, you will hear "My pleasure."

Let's pause for a moment to address some male-centric and misogynistic words and phrases. This phrase pushes my buttons every single time—"resting bitch face." Really? How about "resting asshole man face?" Is that phrase any less offensive?

The common word for women without children is *childless*. When someone refers to me as childless, I'm not; I'm actually "child-free." People often don't consider that the word *less* implies that something is lacking.

How do you feel about this sentence? I've had people say to me, "Does your husband let you do that?" We don't use permission-based language at our house. My husband and I are partners. Can you imagine the impact of the words "let you do" or "make you do" to a woman who has been in a violent or abusive relationship?

Let's dive even deeper into words and their meanings.

What comes to your mind when I say, "They are filthy rich?" When did being rich become filthy? This is another misunderstanding of religious dogma where to be poor is godly and to be rich is filthy. Think of the wealthy people you know who are kind and generous and giving. To me, filthy rich might apply to those who make their money from human trafficking, stealing, or the like.

Coming up is a list of words and phrases in English that embody violence, aggression, and domination. Many of them are literally gang lingo or prison slang. I am sharing the following list with you so that you will begin to consider just what is behind these words. To say it in another way, what is the background of each word, and what has the word come to mean?

Here we go: "World domination," "warriors," "strangle," "knife," "rape," "got your back," "more bang for your buck," and your account has been "terminated." "Fight the flu." "Kill the cancer." "Shred your abs." "Be on the cutting edge." "Scramble to succeed." "He beat me to it." We are facing a "deadline." We "crunch numbers," and we use "bullet points." We receive our "walking papers" and our "military orders." She's just the old "ball and chain." We're told to get married and "settle down." An "alarm" clock wakes us up. A door "buzzes." We've got a "bad back" and a "bum knee." Pregnant women have a "bump." Someone says they are going to give us "tough love."

On most of the crime television shows featuring police investigators, the criminal is usually a man and usually called Mr. Psychopath. The victim of the crime is usually a woman and usually called by her first name. Why is that?

I even discovered these words on my botanical, organic shower gel: "harness," "wind down," and "tackle." Ahhh! I'm not even safe in my own shower!

OK, take a deep breath. Take another breath. Let's shift gears and energy and go to the other end of the spectrum. Let's learn a new word that evokes beauty.

Selmelier. The word was on a salt box, and I was so intrigued that I went to the company's website. I bet you can't wait to learn what this word means. A selmelier helps you choose an appropriate gourmet salt to go with every dish. Mark Bitterman created this clever word to describe what he does. This man knows his salt and knows how to communicate. According to him, "A selmelier is to salt what the sommelier is to wine, providing information and expertise that helps diners and chefs get the best possible results from their food."[2] This word is so lovely that it just might end up in the dictionary!

Bitterman's high-frequency Himalayan pink salt is my favorite. No, I am not getting a kickback (see how aggressive words just pop

---

2   "About Bitterman Salt Co.," Bitterman Salt Co., accessed August 25, 2021, https://bittermansalt.co/pages/about-us.

up—what I meant to say was commission) for promoting his salt. At least not before this book came out!

Now it's your turn to practice beautiful, inclusive language with some eye-opening and heartwarming exercises.

Three Ways to UpLevel Your Communication with Beautiful Language

First, I will share with you two personal tales from my files called "customer service faux pas."

Example 1: I called a nonprofit that I belong to in order to renew my yearly membership. The woman who took my call said, "I can see that you have expired." I laughed and said, "Well, I am pretty sure that I have not expired, but my membership has."

Example 2: I called a company to close my account. The agent kept repeating, "To terminate your account, we have to do the following." Well, hello, is there a death in the family? While I cannot say for sure that they chose the word "terminate" on purpose, I do suspect that they did so to shame me into feeling bad because I was closing my account. Perhaps using this bad language was a scare tactic to try and make more money.

Does your company use fear-based scripts like this? Is your entire customer care team trained and skillful in beautiful, inclusive language?

Take a look at your speaking habits, and think about ways that you can expand your language and bring more good mojo and coop- eration to the workspace by speaking beautifully.

1. Beauty is checking ourselves at the door and considering, "What if I ruin that relationship?" Has this happened to you? What would you do differently the next time around?

2. Avoid language that is aggressive, blaming, or bullying. Such language causes others to be on the defensive and leads to a breakdown in communication.

3. Examine your language to see whether you use words that are directive. Directive words are words that imply giving an order, such as you "must," you "have to," or you are "required to." Also take a look at the over-used wimpy trio—I "should've," I "would've," and I "could've" to see whether they are part of your vernacular.

Three Ways to UpLevel Your Communication with Inclusive Language

1. Begin to think of your communication as a dialogue (a conversation between two or more people), not a monologue (a single speaker).

2. Monitor your use of the word *guys*. Find new ways of expression that welcome and include everyone.

3. Become self-aware and determine whether you are leaving folks out of the conversation by using limiting, small, or masculine-based language.

Using beautiful and inclusive language to communicate will serve you well. You will demonstrate an emotional intelligence and thoughtfulness in your way of speaking. Your business will grow, your relationships will be richer, and employees or coworkers will want to follow your lead. Your project will get funded. You might even save money when your account is "terminated."

And now that you have mastered the art of beautiful and conscious speaking, let's continue. Up next is a chapter designed especially for women. Yes, women do communicate differently. Prepare to learn some exciting new insights about female expression for both women and men. While this next chapter is geared toward women, it's really for everyone, because remember that each human has both female and male energy within.

Using beautiful and inclusive language to communicate will serve you well.

CHAPTER 5

Female Expression and Energy

Never underestimate your female power, for it is your greatest strength.

Years ago I called a travel company to book a vacation. I used the following language, "May I book this trip on this date?" The very serious man with a monotone voice said, "No, you can't. That's not how this works." Now, bear in mind, that I was the customer calling him. After he repeated, "No, you can't" one too many times, I realized that my red hair would catch fire if I did not change my voice and strategy. This person did not attend courtesy school. He didn't speak the language of politeness. He had not been introduced to Mr. Emotional Intelligence. I switched my technique and changed my voice tone to firm and unemotional and said, "I am not asking your permission, I am just that polite. Here is what you're going to do for me." And guess what? He finally did as I asked.

Now let's deconstruct that whole unnecessarily complicated transaction. Basically, my kindness was judged as weakness. Now that's just sad to me. Because, frankly, I envision a world where emotional intelligence, civil communication, and kind conversations are recognized for the strengths that they are. Don't get me wrong: I acknowledge that this level of communication takes more heart. You'll remember from previous chapters that heart is fundamental to my communication philosophy. Your heart has its own intelligence, and interacting with kindness is a great strength. Meaningful conversations that matter *do* take more time, more commitment, and more energy. However, I want to emphasize that cultivating this skill will lead to more personal happiness with relationships both in the workplace and in your personal life. In the workplace, you will simply evaluate what is and is not appropriate. It hurts my heart when I witness executive women who are not speaking up for fear of backlash or getting fired.

> I envision a world where emotional intelligence, civil communication, and kind conversations are recognized for the strengths that they are.

Now, in delightful contrast, I have had many conversations with experienced women who did climb the corporate ladder. They shared with me that their ability to communicate and present well led to their being promoted.

Women, this chapter is written especially for you. Men, this chapter is for you too. It will help you expand your thinking about the voices of professional women. Good communication is good communication, but there are differences in the way women and men express themselves. As you are reading, I encourage you to think about any ways you could be holding yourself back vocally as an executive.

Goethe said, "Let everyone sweep in front of his own door, and the whole world will be clean." I love this saying because it means that I will have a better life if I take responsibility for myself and my actions.

It means knowing what your business *is* and what it is *not*. Changing the world begins at my home, extends into my community, and then beyond. For me, this begins with the way I choose to communicate.

It wasn't always this way for me, and it has not been easy. I grew up in a family that spoke *at* each other, gossiped, and frequently disagreed disagreeably. There were some sharp tongues in my family, especially among the women. What I learned through years of healing and growth was that I was using my voice in the same way, as they were, as a defense mechanism. I was using my words as weapons because that was how I had been spoken to and that was what I had learned. This is a very hurtful and limiting way of speaking.

Here's a fact: studies show that a woman-led company is typically more profitable. The Korn Ferry Institute found that "firms with female CEOs and CFOs produce superior stock price performance, compared to the market average, and firms with high gender diversity on their board of directors are more profitable and larger than firms with low gender diversity, according to a new study from S&P Global Market Intelligence."[3] BBC News also reports that "London-listed companies are more profitable when women make up more than one in three executive roles, according to new research."[4] And to top it off, according to a recently released report from the Credit Suisse Research Institute, "Companies with more female executives in decision-making positions continue to generate stronger market returns and superior profits, and contrary to conventional wisdom,

---

3   Beatrice Grech-Cumbo, "Want Higher Profits? Hire a Female CEO, CFO," Korn Ferry, accessed August 2021, https://www.kornferry.com/insights/this-week-in-leadership/women-ceo-cfo-stock-performance.

4   BBC News, "Firms with More Female Executives 'Perform Better,'" July 27, 2020, https://www.bbc.com/news/business-53548704.

women in leadership roles do not actively exclude other women from promotions to top management."[5]

Impressive reading, right? So here is my question: Why do so many businesswomen speak like men? What I mean is an aggressive, fast manner of speaking with no diplomacy. The way some women speak, you can't tell whether they're women or men. Well, read my lips: you are not a man. Your voice should reflect your female nature. Patriarchy has taught us that our voices are secondary and that we must turn up the masculine aspects of ourselves. This actually does not work well, as you will be working against your natural flow and personal expression. It is energetically incorrect to lower your frequency to something you are not. Ask yourself, Are you turning down your female power? This is like using an artificial sweetener when there is pure, delicious, natural sugar made by Mother Nature herself.

I hear voices that give me pause and are hard to hear. I have heard voices that literally caused me physical pain. Sometimes I hear a woman's voice that is too low to be her ideal pitch. At the other spectrum, I hear fifty-year-old women who speak like children. Sometimes the voice coming out is based on emotions that have never healed or roles in families that have not been moved beyond. For example, a few years ago, I met a woman who was in her fifties who spoke in an artificially soft and very high-pitched tone that sounded like a little girl. I learned that she was raised by her father and still saw herself as "daddy's little girl." Her voice sounded like what I call the "still-seeking-approval voice." Believe me, I get it. I was told to sit down, be still, and be quiet as a child.

---

5   Credit Suisse, "Credit Suisse Research Institute Releases the CS Gender 3000: The Reward for Change Report Analyzing the Impact of Female Representation in Boardrooms and Senior Management," September 22, 2016, https://www.credit-suisse. com/us/en/articles/media-releases/csri-gender-3000-201609.html.

According to the British newspaper *The Telegraph*, Margaret Thatcher went from a "'shrill' housewife to Downing Street."[6] The former prime minister took voice lessons in the 1970s from Stewart Pearce, a famous voice coach in the UK who has worked with many celebrities and luminaries, to make her voice sound "firmer and more powerful." If you have heard her before voice training and after voice training, you will notice a substantial difference in her pitch, voice quality, and delivery. In the same *Telegraph* article, Stewart Pearce shares this about working with Ms. Thatcher: "I gave her gravity and weight so that she could be taken seriously." And, according to him, "She was charming, kind, immensely intelligent. Intimidatingly intelligent."

Your voice is your branding. Women, I want you to understand that a too-high-pitched tone of voice will never be taken seriously in the workplace. It possesses no self-understanding, no maturity, and it makes it hard for us to feel you have credibility. If you are stuck in only your Maiden voice, it's time to shift the gears. You have so much more to offer the world.

Here's another story for you. Years ago, when I was just a young pup, I worked for a retail store where folks sent faxes (remember those?), made copies, and shipped boxes worldwide. The owners were a couple—a very tall couple. He had been in the military, and she was a military wife and mother. The woman, I will call her Cindy, was over six feet tall, with long strawberry-blond hair, big glasses, and a tiny high-pitched voice. Many times people thought that I was the owner. What were people picking up on? The difference between Cindy and me entailed two things. The first was my voice, and the second was

---

6   Bill Gardner, "From 'Shrill' Housewife to Downing Street: The Changing Voice of Margaret Thatcher," *The Telegraph*, November 25, 2014, https://www.telegraph.co.uk/news/politics/11251919/From-shrill-housewife-to-Downing-Street-the-changing-voice-of-Margaret-Thatcher.html.

my energy/presence. Customers would have no way of knowing our backgrounds or education levels: they were simply reacting to those two aspects of how I showed up and how I spoke.

If you believe that you are somehow less than everyone else and you use a voice that reflects this belief, you have become just another cog in the patriarchal train. Ouch! Women's self-hatred runs rampant and is also heavily denied. I invite each of you to study Iyanla Vanzant's wisdom around why women treat other women badly. Iyanla is a very accomplished author and inspirational speaker who has a fantastic TV show called *Iyanla, Fix My Life* on OWN. If you want to watch someone cut through all the bullshit and demonstrate in-your-face-absolute-fierce love, watch her show.

Another person I love on this topic is professor and researcher Dr. Brené Brown. Dr. Brown has rich data in her books about vulnerability and belonging. In her words, she is a "researcher, storyteller, Texan." She speaks about "the critic" and why we do not want to listen to them. When I was performing as a singer, I could not believe the criticism wielded at me. Ninety-nine percent of the time, this advice came from nonmusicians. Why should I listen to folks who don't have the courage to perform but only give *unsolicited* advice to those who do? You see, I am no longer interested in people who will not take risks. Reading Dr. Brown's books has shifted my belief system. I feel her books will cause a shift in your beliefs that can be a pathway to a richer and more effective voice. Our job now is to continue to heal and arrive at honest communication for ourselves and every other woman (and man).

It's simple: if you are the boss and people don't think you are the boss when you speak, you are losing traction and influence. If you constantly defer to men, you will never truly lead in the boardroom or Zoom room.

People have said to me, "But you can't change your voice." I don't know where that belief came from, but of course you can change your voice. You can change your clothes. You can change your mind. You can build a richer, healthier voice with more carrying power and impact for good.

Now, the kind of voice you have will be related to the kind of energy you project. But what is energy exactly? We can't see it, but we can feel it. There are people with strong energy that we can feel and people with so little energy or life force that it gives new meaning to the word *wallflower*. In the laws of nature, we are only one of two things: growing or dying. Energy, to me, is that charisma, that attractiveness that draws us to a person. It is sex appeal. It is thinking that our conversation will be fascinating. It's that "it" factor that many celebrities and entrepreneurs have. It is a person comfortable in their skin. It is a person who knows what they stand for and does not apologize for it. It is the essence of a person that has that sparkle, that joie de vivre that we want to be around, learn from, and follow.

We don't always have an accurate picture of our own self or our abilities. One time, I had an audition for a television commercial, and three things happened. Number one, it was the only time I forgot my headshot. Number two, I thought I'd done a really, really bad job. Number three, I booked that commercial, and it was one of the most successful and fun acting roles I ever had.

Have you ever been on an airplane and a big dude comes in and has the seat next to you? Yes, he stuffs that oversized bag in the overhead compartment and slams his body in the seat. Next, his feet are pretty much over the boundary into your personal space and his arms all over the arm rests. Those arm rests are meant to be shared, people. Men, I applaud you, (although it's annoying to be sitting next to you on a plane) because many of you take up space all day. You have strong energy and don't apologize for it.

Now, have you ever been on an airplane and a woman enters? She has the seat next to you. She places her bag in the overhead compartment. She says "I'm sorry" at least three times while carefully making herself as small as possible to get to the seat beyond you. She literally seems to be apologizing for the very act of taking up air or space. Women, stop it! I'm not kidding—stop it! Stop apologizing for taking up space or for having a voice. You matter. Stop saying, "I'm sorry." If you must climb over me simply say, "Excuse me" or "Please excuse me." Here ends the lecture for today!

Your job as a leader is to know what type of energy is primary for you. Are you a thinker, feeler, innovator, or visionary? I have found throughout my life that personality tests, self-introspection, and time spent with those who truly know me are the keys to unleashing this. My own personal superpowers are intuition and creative problem solving. My problem solving is interdisciplinary and multipassionate. I draw from all my life experience, from jobs I've had, from my curiosity about everything, from places I've lived (twelve so far!), and from masters I've studied with. A leader who has strong energy and confidence can work the room, conversing with folks from all walks of life. A CEO with strong energy and confidence makes us buy into the company's mission, purpose, product, or service.

Now, let's talk for a minute about voice production and energy. Did you know the first microphones that resemble the ones we have today were not invented until 1916? Singers had to understand and learn resonance so that their voice would carry all the way to the back row. When I studied voice as an undergrad with my German opera coach, Dr. Calder, we did not use microphones. When I first began studying with her, she came very close to me and I could not believe the power and volume she had in her voice. I am not sure I had ever heard a voice that powerful and loud before. She had been a professional opera singer in Europe before she and her husband left Nazi Germany for the freedom of the United States. We were expected to learn the art of correct vocal production and cultivate the stamina and energy needed to do so. Being an opera singer has been compared to having the stamina of a fighter pilot.

Now that we've had a romp through the unique qualities of the female voice and energy, I've got some exercises for you to apply in your role as an executive.

Three Ways to UpLevel Your Communication with Your Female Voice

Men, don't be afraid to explore this aspect of yourself! We all have both female and male DNA.

I encourage you to go deep on this one—get ahold of yourself. This may be a part of the book where you might have to radically change something about your voice. I have women say to me, "Nobody ever told me that anything was wrong with my voice." I am not suggesting that anything is "wrong." I *am* saying that there may be room for growth or development. You simply have to acknowledge the truth and be willing to change.

Over the years, I have met many professional women, and I can immediately tell that they are not being promoted because of their speaking voice. They have not yet found their true voice. There are many reasons why people won't tell you *it's your voice*. Folks may be embarrassed, they may feel that they would hurt you, they may want your job and be jealous of you so they will *not* tell you, they may have a hearing challenge, or they may think you just won't accept the feedback. It's vulnerable ground because our voice is within us and it's personal. It can be hard to hear that our voice is hard to hear (pun totally intended).

1. Audio record yourself, and really listen. Do not judge—just assess. Does your voice say what you think it does? Does it cause you to lean in or move away? Would *you* take this voice tone seriously?

2. Does your voice feel good? Is it easy to produce? Remember that your voice is a physical thing. Here is a simple (not easy) exercise that will allow you to feel the vibrations created by your voice. You want to *feel* this, not *think* this. Place two fingers from each hand on each side of your nose to feel the vibration. Now open your teeth slightly, close your lips, and say "mmm-hmm," feeling that it comes from the front of your face. Begin at the pitch that feels natural to you. Next allow your jaw to relax by dropping it, open your mouth more, and expand into the sounds "ah-hah, yes," again feeling that it comes from the front of your face. This exercise gives you an indicator of the pitch range that you should naturally be speaking from.

3. Examine your mindset. Do you believe you have nothing to say, or do you know your voice and your purpose in the world? Have you been told as a woman "Be quiet," "Your voice doesn't matter," or "We don't want to hear from you"?

Oh yes, women, most of us have much work to do around this. I want you to create a personal declaration to begin to override the programming that has occurred throughout your life. If you find that you need therapy or counseling, please seek out a qualified professional to help you.

"What I have to say matters."

Here are some suggestions that I have for you. Say these sentences to yourself every day as an affirmation of truth and change:

- "What I have to say matters."
- "I am here to contribute and serve."
- "Dammit, I have something to say!"
- "I am building a voice that can be heard right now."
- "People want to hear from me."
- "I may be more of an introvert, but I easily say what needs to be said."

Three Ways to UpLevel Your Communication with Your Unique Energy

1. Do you resort to turning down your volume, or do you find yourself doing habits like upspeak when you are in high-stake situations? Upspeak is when your pitch at the end of a sentence goes up instead of down. Upspeak is a negative thing that is very different from UpLeveling or upgrading your speech. When you upspeak it sounds like you are not sure of yourself or that you are asking questions. Your pitch needs to come down like a period to end a sentence. No question marks, no commas, no semicolons, but a period. Imagine this: giant question

marks coming from your mouth and floating around in the air. As a result, we feel unsure—does she know what she is talking about? Can we trust her?

2. Clients have said to me, "I am fine with my employees; it's the board I get nervous in front of." Or "My coworkers are easy to present to, but I am completely intimidated by our CEO." What you need to do when this happens is exactly the opposite of becoming smaller or contracting. You need to be bigger and take up more space. This can mean finding a stronger posture, sitting tall in your chair, and becoming aware of your vocal volume.

   Think about when you feel at your best or are most confident. If that doesn't work within a few minutes, think about something or someone you dearly love. Folks, this is not a thinking exercise; this is a feeling exercise. When you think of being at your best, being in your zone, you should notice your energy shifting. You should feel better, perhaps more whole or happier.

   For me, three feel-good times are after I work out, share a meal with a dear friend, or work with a client. And this is the strong and positive energy that you want to bring to your communication as a business professional.

3. Warm up physically before you speak or lead a meeting. Our voice is physical, so we need to warm up. You should also warm up before running, before racing a car, or before climbing a mountain.

I invite you to:

- Gently shake your entire body, including your face and lips, for about thirty seconds.

- Prepare and practice before meetings. Listen, I have been performing and speaking for too many years to even tell you how many. A couple years ago, I decided to kind of wing it on a live stage and didn't do my usual prep time. I was not at all happy with my results. I did not show up fully. I was way too nervous and did not connect with my audience or attract the new clients that I "should" have. In fact, I had one giant pause as I forgot my words. I was just relieved when it was over. Boo. Hiss. I missed my opportunity to delight, influence, and impact my audience.

Ah, how fun was this exploration? For some, their female voice could be their superpower, while others will choose humor to delight their audience as a means of effective communication.

Prepare to be inspired as I share with you ways to delight your audience in chapter 6.

Delight Your Audience

Charm, humor, and keepin' it real will delight an audience.

It seems like only yesterday. I remember feeling so eloquent and fluent as I gave an interview on a Zoom call. And then it happened—I stumbled over a word. I'm not sure which word I stumbled over, but you can imagine I am a stickler for correct pronunciation. But guess what? I didn't make a big deal out of it. Instead, I activated one of my superpowers: the Miluna chuckle! Then I said dryly, "It took a PhD for me to mispronounce that word."

I should explain that this phrase is one of my go-to phrases. My sense of humor is pretty dry and borders on irreverence depending on my audience. You might not be aware of what type of humor comes naturally to you. Is it slapstick, dark, silly, or empathetic? Ask a good friend; they'll be able to tell you.

So let's look at what happens when you use your humor and laugh at yourself. First, your audience realizes that you are comfortable with yourself and that you trip over your words just like they do. We

We all stumble—it doesn't mean we are less than; it means we are human.

all stumble—it doesn't mean we are less than; it means we are human. I have heard very successful CEOs whom I admire mispronounce words. Your audience, in turn, becomes more comfortable. Over the course of my career, one of the biggest truths I've noticed is that the CEOs and leaders who touch our hearts are willing and able to use funnies in the workplace or boardroom.

One of the main keys to using humor in business is discerning what is appropriate. For example, I like to cuss sometimes. I know! You are all terribly shocked by that statement. But listen to this: sometimes a well-placed curse word is just the thing you need to make a point or an impact. Of course, for many workplaces, cussing is not appropriate. If I am speaking to any religious group, for example, cussing is not appropriate. Likewise, if I were in front of an audience that happens to be deaf I would choose my jokes or funny stories very carefully, knowing that they will be delivered in sign language or with captions. This situation is similar to telling jokes in different languages: they don't always translate, and they're not always funny.

What do I mean by "delight your audience"? The word *delight*, according to *Merriam-Webster*, means "joy," "extreme satisfaction," or "something that gives great pleasure." And words that relate to *delight* include *treat, contentment, entertain, enchant, amuse, wow*, and *thrill*. And ask yourself this, When was the last time you attended a presentation that thrilled you? A presentation that knocked your socks off? Many times I find that my clients underestimate the power they have to enchant their audience. They seem almost afraid to use their power. I mean, "Gracious, what will others think?"

Well, here is where I am going to pull over for a short interlude because I have an extremely important message for you. Are you sitting comfortably? OK, here goes: *stop using FOOPO right now!*

FOOPO is a Miluna-ism and means "fear of other people's opinions." I know all about it because I operated most of my life that way. Fear of criticism. Fear of what other people would say or do. It's what I was taught: "What will the neighbors think?" What I discovered along the way was that most people didn't know me well enough to give a solid opinion or feedback. So give yourself a break! FOOPO will simply exhaust you and make you timid. I'm not suggesting that you throw your diplomacy or courtesy out the window. I *am* saying that most other folks will be in no position to understand your purpose or mission and that their opinion (if they are not a friend or in your inner circle) should not carry that much weight. There is only one of you, and you must live your best life.

I shared in chapter 5 that I am a trained opera singer. I'm also a jazz singer, and back in the '90s, I sang in jazz and blues clubs in Virginia, Maryland, and Washington, DC. I love old jazz tunes because they can be very suggestive and naughty when you figure out what the lyrics really mean. One of my favorite songs is "Peel Me a Grape" (Peel me a grape / Crush me some ice / Skin me a peach), a very provocative song, and when I would lean in and get close to some of the men in the audience, they would shrink back. I was surprised to find that lots of men were nervous and embarrassed and completely missed my seduction. Listen, men, you were supposed to enjoy it! Live a little! Share in the fun! I'm not planning to invite you to go home with me!

This experience of performing in nightclubs taught me just how uncomfortable many people are with emotions or feelings or anything that did not come from their rational mind. But remember, you are so much more than your mind. Your mind may lie to you to protect you, just as the ego keeps you small (because you are always worrying what people are thinking about you). The ego's job is to protect you from pain, and it relies only on past experiences.

Yet we love show business. Supertalented and hardworking singers, actors, poets, and dancers help us feel alive, put us in touch with our emotions, change our perspective, and dazzle us with their abilities. One of the most meaningful performances I ever witnessed was our Christmas concert at a tiny theater in New Jersey many years ago. It was just a small community theater where you acted and brought food and invited every single one of your friends and family. One of our singers delivered a song in tribute to his father, who had just passed away. It hit me hard because my father had passed away in an automobile crash when I was seven years old. To this day, I still miss my father and imagine the conversations that we would have. This singer's performance brought me immediately back to my personal grief. And the real magic of his singing was that he allowed his tears to flow while he was performing. His crying did not interfere with his voice, just added many layers to his song. The fact that he would share his vulnerability and pain was his gift to the audience. Performers are comfortable with drama. But this type of drama is very different from being a so-called drama queen in your daily life. As a matter of fact, I think that phrase could be added to my avoid-these-words-and-phrases list near the end of chapter 4!

I have noticed that many high achievers and successful company owners become so single-minded that they lose their emotional compass. Some might argue that this is necessary to build an empire. I agree that drive, focus, and time are needed to play at that level. The problems come up later when a lack of emotional intelligence, especially in communication, leads to a break down in professional and personal relationships. To me, emotions are like messengers giving me insights and opportunities. If you can no longer access your emotional body, you are missing important clues and information. You may have lost your ability to sense when someone else could be hurt or offended by what you say or how you say it. If you want to move beyond doing transactional business and having shallow relationships, you must grow your emotional intelligence.

Let's talk more about some of the elements that add up to delight your audience. It may be telling a personal story, sharing a funny anecdote, or a heartwarming tale about one of your rip-roaring failures! Your style may be reciting some shocking facts, numbers, or data. If you are an author, read from your own book. What the audience wants is to hear from YOU, not have you turn around reading your PowerPoint slides. We don't care about your deck; you could have emailed us your deck to read. We want to know things like: What is this talk going to do for me? Why are you in business? What have you learned? What do you stand for? A great presenter *always* makes it personal.

> **If you want to move beyond doing transactional business and having shallow relationships, you must grow your emotional intelligence.**

When I lived in Los Angeles, I had the pleasure of attending a lecture and book signing at the American Jewish University. The lecture was introducing a new book from an opera singer who happened to be blind. Her name is Laurie Rubin, and her book is *Do You Dream in Color? Insights from a Girl without Sight*. She was extraordinary: an opera singer, writer, and jewelry designer (yes, a blind jewelry designer), and she was strong and confident. To my eyes, she resembled Barbra Streisand. Amazingly, she could describe every color and "see" what things looked like in her mind. Lest you doubt that colors can be felt or your imagination is real, tell me how a blind woman can "see" colors just like I can? I mean, you can't see love, but I sure hope that you can feel it! Einstein himself said, "The true sign of intelligence is not knowledge but imagination."

Why do most of us love TED Talks so much? Well, it's usually because those chosen TED Talkers have something original or captivating to say. They have a perspective that perhaps no one else has presented. They change our mindset and challenge our beliefs. They work to enroll us in their movement, their crusade. These folks usually have strong opinions and strong solutions. We don't want to hear the same old information in the same old way. Understand, even if it *is* information that we already know, it can and should be presented in a way that only *you* can come up with!

Have you ever read Dr. Seuss? I bet that he was criticized over his writing at the beginning of his career especially. The man was a genius—who thinks or talks like that? How about the extremely scary novels from prolific Stephen King? Who can forget *Carrie* or *Christine*? I confess, I can't read them anymore because my overactive imagination conjures up something even worse (I won't share details here in the event that you are headed off to bed)! Fun fact: I hear that Mr. King is a very nice person when you meet him!

I also loved the book by Scott Hartley entitled *The Fuzzy and the Techie: Why the Liberal Arts Will Rule the Digital World*. Mr. Hartley heard the words *fuzzy* and *techie* as a student at Stanford University. Those who studied humanities or social sciences were considered a fuzzy and those who studied computer or hard sciences were considered a techie. Now that we are entering, or returning to, the Age of Aquarius (each astrological age lasts approximately 2,160 years), those who are creative and artistic will thrive. The Age of Aquarius also represents a desire to just help others. Take heart, all my liberal arts–educated ones, your skills will now be en vogue! Take note, if you are a boss, you would be wise to hire a few more graduates of the humanities now. Last night I was on a Zoom video call with my friend in New York City who is in the cybersecurity space. He said that he would hire people with liberal arts degrees who could learn to code in a couple of languages. For him, the liberal arts curriculum builds the critical thinking skills and heart needed to excel at his company.

One of my best friends told me, "You shouldn't go around Silicon Valley saying that you're a 'fuzzy.'" That should have been my first clue that I was in the wrong place at the wrong time. The truth is I speak both fuzzy and techie! I read my husband's *IEEE* (Institute of Electrical and Electronics Engineers) *Spectrum* magazine. I love cars, especially race cars. I love the sound and acoustics of the engine and can tell them apart by how they sound speeding down the road in front of my house. You don't have to be either-or; you can bridge both and make a difference for humanity and our planet.

Don't be afraid to stand out from the crowd.

Don't be afraid to stand out from the crowd. And I give you permission to do so in this chapter! Another very important thing to remember is that the show must go on. When you stumble or make a "mistake" while presenting or speaking, simply acknowledge it. Don't ignore it or make a big deal out of it. If you make a big deal out of it, you draw more attention to it. If you are off your game, shift your attention to the bottom of your feet and take a deep breath. Don't lose even one member of your audience. Every. Single. One. of them matters. Your job is to be inclusive, meaning that you speak to and include every person in your audience. I invite you to envision that you hold each precious person that is listening to and/or watching you in the palm of your hands. It is both your responsibility and your joy to do so. When you do this, you will enjoy public speaking and presenting *so* much more!

Three Ways to UpLevel Your Communication by Delighting Your Audience

1. Go back to your notes (because I have no doubt that you are doing the homework in my book, right?) and pull out all the reasons and intentions for each speech or presentation that you deliver. How can you delight your audience? First, you must research and know the group, and that will point you in the right direction. You may have to test your approach a couple times, just like comedians do. Comedy is brutal. The best comedians test their jokes in comedy clubs and with live audiences to determine the success of their humor. If it's funny, we will laugh.

2. Discover what is charming or funny about you. Some of you seem scared to be funny or are unfamiliar with "funny," especially in the business world. I have found that women especially have anxiety about releasing their inner comedian because we've been told we're not funny. You can throw that lie in the trash along with FOOPO! Your speech could instead be focused on facts delivered with a sense of irony or bringing data to life by painting a picture (think adjectives, think qualities, think colors, and use highly descriptive words—become your own Picasso). Developing your self-awareness and imagination will help you begin to turn the corner and transform you into a more engaging and much better presenter.

3. Study the most watched TED Talks on YouTube, and learn what the speaker is doing to bring us into their world. What do you love about them? Is it their voice?

Their message? The way they speak? Their body language? The way they make a funny face? What makes their talk compelling? What makes you watch until the end? On the other end of the spectrum, what makes you stop watching?

Compelling public speaking is all about delighting your audience, but you must also know how to properly make introductions and lead a meeting, be it in real life or via a computer or phone. Go ahead and keep reading to dive right into chapter 7.

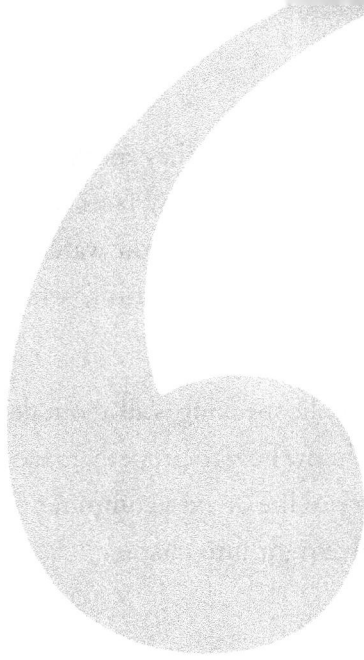

The Brave New World of Introductions and Leading Virtually

You must radiate more energy and attention for virtual meetings.

The world has changed. Zoom has become a commonly used verb, like Google. The pandemic has required us to meet with clients and hold meetings in relative isolation from our homes. This trend seems sure to continue. I know that conducting meetings from your home office can seem challenging. Distractions range from needing to answer the doorbell to sign for a package to the cat walking your keyboard with its fuzzy tail tickling your face!

Set up your environment for success so that you look good.

Do not fear, because I've got some savvy techniques and strategies to share with you on how to lead meetings that other people will want to attend! Here's one of my first pieces of advice: set up your environment for success so that you look good.

Don't make me look at that otherworldly moving virtual backdrop that makes your head disappear every few seconds. This is your chance to show us something interesting about yourself, to have something on display that can be a conversation starter.

Here are some ideas I have for you, along with some examples I have seen that work well. Think of yourself as a Hollywood set designer—you get to create a professional atmosphere that reflects your personality.

- A desk, table, or credenza behind you with a vase of flowers or one stunning sculpture

- The book that you wrote tastefully displayed on the bookshelf behind you

- A stunning piece of artwork on the wall behind you (I have a colleague who uses a standing desk and mounted three gorgeous pieces of art on the wall behind her.)

- Bookshelves neatly filled with books and interesting objets d'art

- Custom or branded virtual Zoom backgrounds that are simple and easy on the eyes

- Shelves arranged to display your jewelry, artwork, or other items you sell (Take a look at Etsy or Instagram for creative ways to display them.)

- A custom backdrop for a professional photographer using her photos (of course)

- A mannequin fully dressed in a clothing designer's latest outfit

- A room divider that you love decorated to reflect your company or store

∽ A custom sign or banner well placed behind you or hanging on the wall

∽ If I were the owner of a winery, I would elegantly display three or four bottles of my wine behind me

Now record yourself with your background. Look with a critical, objective eye (or two), and see how everything appears from a video camera perspective.

Get a second opinion. Schedule a meeting with a friend or your spouse, or invite your Chihuahua to a Zoom meeting. Ask them to share what your background is saying about you. Don't wait until ten minutes before your meeting and risk showing up in a less-than-professional way.

First, I really, really, really (is that strong enough?) encourage you to put your camera on. I know—you may be wearing pajamas with little pink bunnies on them. During the meeting may be the only time you have to grab a snack. I get it. Just turn your camera off while eating and then back on. Set a company policy insisting that people turn on their cameras. You could even reimburse employees up to a certain dollar amount to purchase equipment that works well. It makes it very hard on others to determine your level of participation when they can't see you. It inhibits our ability to feel a connection and work with you when we don't have visuals. What if you have folks in the crowd who are deaf? In addition, if you are a quiet person *and* not on camera, you risk becoming invisible to the powers that be.

To have participation from most or all of your team, instead of just the extroverts,

> **To have participation from most or all of your team, instead of just the extroverts, create a system for folks to speak up.**

create a system for folks to speak up. Best practice is to put out the agenda the day before with specifics, including the names of people in charge of each line item. Know that items that require discussion will always pop up during a meeting. Within Zoom, people could click on the applause button or another button and that is your cue to call on them. As a fearless leader, you also ensure your colleagues get to speak, stay on track, and stay on time.

Folks, we gotta see your entire face on those *Hollywood Squares*! Ideally, give us 75 to 80 percent of yourself showing up. We want to see you from midchest or just above the waist if you are sitting. If you are standing, we should see a nice perspective of you (again, check this by recording yourself, and then make any necessary adjustments). It can be hard to hear others for many reasons. Poor-quality speakers, not enough volume control, soft-spoken folks, and people talking while they think they are on mute (yes, I forget too). This makes it even more important that I see your entire face so that I can read your lips along with hearing you. I have a friend who had a stroke, and part of his comprehension depends on being able to read lips.

The "eyes" have it. We need solid eye contact, especially here in the United States. Strong eye contact demonstrates confidence and engagement. Your eyes should be mostly to camera or moving back and forth from the person you are looking at to camera. I make strong eye contact into the camera, look intently at the other person, and back to camera. This is because I have a pro camera mounted on the top of my PC. If you have a laptop with a built-in camera, this eliminates the need to look back and forth. I recommend that you look away to the side (10 percent of the time) when thinking or making a point. This creates a balance between not enough and too much eye contact and also gives your eyes a rest.

Here's a special tip for my women reading this book. Studies show that we must still earn our place at the meeting. Folks don't seem to know why we are there unless we tell them (no, I can't make this stuff up). Having said that, it serves you best to state your first and last name, your title, and a few concise words about your purpose at each meeting.

Likewise, there seems to be a trend for dropping titles these days. You may think titles don't matter, and they don't, mostly. However, I hope you're sitting down because I have quite a bit to say about titles. We all know people with massive titles that go on for days who are not leaders at all. They are only leaders based on their education, connections, or schmoozing. Personally, I chose to get an advanced degree and never stop learning. I wanted the exceptional path, not the path of the average person.

My degrees don't automatically make me a leader, but they demonstrate my commitment to growth, active study, and the application of knowledge to better my life.

Wow—that reminds me of the unbelievably sexist music literature professor from the UK (yes, he had a doctorate) at Indiana State University who said to me, "Why are you here? You just need to go home and get married." Ha! He obviously had no idea of my capabilities.

What does it mean to introduce others? It means that you are in a position to or have accepted a leadership role. This is not the time to skip over, make fun, or give sloppy introductions because you are not in your power. The audience will think less of you for it. You are the authority, so act like it! Enjoy the role that you have: you get to set the tone, or the atmosphere, for your meeting.

I invite you to completely change your thinking and approach to the art of introducing others. Think of making an introduction as an honor. Be generous with your introduction. This is an opportunity not only to demonstrate your leadership savvy but also to acknowledge others. When you come across as a generous person, people will like you. What you put out there will circle back around to you. And if you can shine the light on others, you truly are a powerful person.

Practice opening your meetings with a warm and inclusive welcome. I know that you will never again (pinkie-swear promise me) use the word *guys* after reading my book! Here are some inclusive meeting openers: "Welcome, everyone"; "Welcome, all"; "Welcome, fantastic folks"; "Welcome, sales team"; or "Good morning, everybody." If you are a small and mighty group, simply greet each person by name. Then, remind folks of the overall intention or purpose of the meeting and that you will be sticking to the agenda and duration of the meeting. Invite everyone to your party, to your world: "Let's talk about how we're going to build this platform."

Think of how you feel when you help others or even witness someone helping another person. Polly Campbell, author of *Imperfect Spirituality*, reported this in *Psychology Today*, "The newest research shows that not only is our mood elevated when we witness kindness, but we act more altruistic ourselves."[7] I personally believe we are wired to be kind, both to ourselves and others. Marianne Williamson says: "The way of the miracle-worker is to see all human behavior as one of two things: either love, or a call for love."

Here's another good reason to learn the art of making formal introductions: the world is bigger than the United States. I was speaking to a friend of mine who owns a successful translation and international marketing company. He shared this with me: if, for

---

7   Polly Campbell, "How Watching a Good Deed Elevates and Inspires," *Psychology Today*, July 15, 2013, https://www.psychologytoday.com/us/blog/imperfect-spirituality/201307/how-watching-good-deed-elevates-and-inspires.

example, you are doing business in Dubai and you mispronounce the other person's name or drop off their title, you will be promptly escorted away by the staff. Your success in business depends on your relationship-building skills and your ability to communicate with respect as you interact within the global community.

Now, let's talk video etiquette. Remember, the following items are magnified on video: eating, chewing gum, getting up frequently, walking around with your computer, playing with your hair, continually stroking your beard or mustache, pushing up your glasses repeatedly, resting your head in your hands, falling asleep, playing with your dog so you're distracted, and talking on the phone to your therapist. The general rule is if you wouldn't do it in person, don't do it on camera.

And etiquette is actually very simple. If I introduce myself as "Dr. Miluna," you call me "Dr. Miluna." Manners are not designed to be cumbersome. They are designed to have people think well of you and give you the confidence to do business with folks outside your usual circles.

Here are a few additional ideas to assist you in being effective when gathering in person:

1. Determine the power seat in the room when you are leading a meeting. Ideally, it would be at an end of the table where you can easily see who is coming in the door. The king or queen always sits in the end chairs. You could also position yourself on the side of the table where the key leadership and influencers would sit right across from you. You want to ensure that you are seen and heard and responded to.

2. If you are presenting, you want to "cheat out." This is an acting technique that means you never turn your back to the

audience (OK, almost never. Sometimes a scene *will* call for this). You are pivoting your body from side to side, facing forward, and never going farther than into a sideways profile. Around ten years ago I was attending a seminar in Newport Beach, California, at the office of a famous "brain doctor." It was a subject that I was eager to learn—maintaining a healthy brain. After having my head cut open to remove the tumor years ago, my brain became extremely important to me! One of the clinic's psychologists was presenting to the room and spent the whole time with his back to me. Yes, the whole time. The man was clueless that a quarter of the room was completely left out. It made me feel like I didn't matter, and I wondered why the doctor didn't have his staff trained in the art of presenting. Why should I pay for a seminar like that?

3. If the meeting is held in a room with a table, keep your hands on the table where we can see them. We don't trust people when we can't see what they're doing with their hands. Are they secretly texting or passing love notes under the table?

I once spoke at a luncheon meeting for a women's group that I used to belong to. The group was far from professional. I was surprised by the patriarchal bravado among some of the women. My speaking topic was "How to Be Heard in a World That Interrupts Women," and I had provided, well in advance, a written introduction to the meeting host, yet I was misintroduced. My name was reduced to "Miluna."

Professionally I am known as "Dr. Miluna," and I can assure you that I have earned my PhD. Would you call a male doctor or any other professional by their first name? It is not arrogant to want my title used; it is a matter of respect.

When I was raised, we didn't yet have *Ms.* I was taught to call people by *Mr.* or *Mrs.* or *Dr.* It is best practice in today's world to call folks by *Mr.* or *Ms.* or *Dr. Mrs.* is a manmade version labeling a woman as married, separating her from the rest of women. *Mr.* implies a male person and nothing more, so *Ms.* is the equivalent for a female person. You all know by now that I am a passionate advocate for equality in communication. In a professional setting, it is nobody's business whether a woman is married.

Here's a special note on introducing folks who identify as something else. Instead of committing a faux pas, don't address the person using any pronoun, but simply use their name or ask what they would like to be called.

And don't listen to folks who say things like, "Well, I am just aggressive. Get over it." Or "I don't have time for all this nice stuff." Actually, you can't afford not to have time. Aggression is not a great strategy, because it doesn't always work. It does not work in all arenas and certainly not with all people. The same thing can be said about harshness. You

If you are the CEO and getting paid the huge bucks, you need to get training in the areas of communication, candor, emotional intelligence, and vulnerability.

want to build the skill of being sensitive enough to deliver what is appropriate in each circumstance. If you are the CEO and getting paid the huge bucks, you need to get training in the areas of communication, candor, emotional intelligence, and vulnerability. We want to trust your leadership.

Now, let's get back to that meeting introduction. My introduction contained my experience as an actor. I was called an actress. Well, I object. I am an actor, defined as a "person who acts."

I am keenly sensitive to words that I believe have been created to imply a lesser person, or a mere female person in the male-dominated world of show business. As a female jazz singer, I was often accused of having less musical prowess than instrumentalists, most of whom were male. My reply was always, "But I always have my instrument with me." And while we're on the topic of putting women down by not using their correct titles, I'm reminded of an article I read recently. First Lady Jill Biden (that's Dr. Jill Biden to you!) was called "kiddo" by a male Northwestern University professor. I mean, dude, really? What century do you live in?

Speaking of professors, for those of you who are educators, I believe that your students will think better of you by formally addressing you by your title. You are not their friend; you are their teacher and ally.

The third transgression from the women's group meeting host was that she mispronounced my last name. Personally, I've heard myself called "Myluna" and "Fahsh," all the way to "Foosh." It is for this very reason that I supply a well written and branded introduction ahead of time, including the correct pronunciation of my name (which, for the record, is "Míloona Fowsh"). Don't make fun of others or give sloppy introductions because you are not in your power. You're not my pal; you're a professional.

OK, folks, thanks for staying with me for that entire exhibition! Take a breath, and let's continue with a few more words about introductions.

Speaking of introductions and making everyone feel included, I have served on several boards for professional women's associations and nonprofits over the years. If you are head of a nonprofit and you have board members, ensure that you are introducing each one of us.

I have been on the advisory board of a nonprofit for five years now, and I have yet to be introduced at the yearly celebration or large gathering. Now, I am honored to be on the board and give willingly of my time, energy, and heart, but I also expect to be acknowledged (at least a couple of times a year). It is not my ego that needs to be named; it is my heart and my fierce need to contribute. Remember, generous introductions lead to generous donations!

At the very least, if there are many folks serving on your board simply create a scrolling slideshow of all of your board members. By doing this the audience can see all those who work behind the scenes. You can even set the scroll speed to fast! The main objective is to say thank you to your hardworking board members—and it's also just good business.

Three Ways to UpLevel Your Communication When Leading Meetings

1. Find a signature way to open and close your meetings that makes people feel welcome and valuable and leaves 'em wanting to come back to next week's meeting. Define what a successful meeting means to you and how you feel afterward.

2. Practice how you will specifically acknowledge your team or colleagues. Pick one person each time to call out with something that moved the company forward. Maybe your SVP did a rock star presentation that attracted two new potential clients. Tell your SVP exactly what was exceptional about her presentation or client meeting. Two examples are (1) "You spoke of our company's vision with

such heart that I felt tears come to my eyes" and (2) "The way you wrapped up that meeting with such clarity was brilliant."

3. Write down how you want to show up for meetings. Here are some questions you could ask yourself: How do you want to be known in your company? What type of communicator do you want to be? What words will you use to communicate your values and goals? What type of communication will you put in place to support your folks (written messages, phone calls, one-on-one video chats, or shared platforms such as Slack or Google Docs)?

Three Ways to UpLevel Your Communication When Introducing Others

1. Use the introduction given to you, or request four key things from the person who will speak. Let them give you highlights of what they would like you to share. Use what was given to you, and then add a few specific words about the person. Do you know them personally? Is there something (appropriately) funny or heartwarming you could share in just a couple moments?

2. Stand or sit up tall with a strong posture that reflects your authority and enthusiasm.

3. Since shaking hands may be on the way out, you could raise your hands in the air implying "air high fives" or briefly do an elbow bump if appropriate. This could be for

an employee's birthday or a celebration of the company's growth with the CEO.

Enjoy this brave new world of "virtuality" and clear communication, while staying true to who you are and to your company's mission.

When you show up as charismatic and generous, you will also be perceived as more attractive. And as a result, your sales and income will automatically go up. Business is all about building relationships that count and can outlast trends.

Let's jump into chapter 8 and talk about how to build better relationships and increase business.

Building Relationships Matters and Leads to More Business

Find one area of commonality to connect to others.

On a daily basis, I get multiple messages over social media from businesspeople seeking clients that start something like this, "Hey, Miluna—what do you do?" or "What are you up to?" or this latest gem from Facebook, "Would you be a foot model for my product?" Let me explain why this is not a good idea. First, I really don't appreciate your casual tone. Second, why are you asking me what my business is? It's your job to find out! Let's turn things around, and allow me to ask you some questions: Did you read my profile or watch any of my videos? Did you spend any time at all researching me? Yet you want to know what my business is? Well, I will do my best to respond to you while remaining polite and respectful, but an approach with zero preparation and no understanding of what I'm about will never earn my business. Well done, (said in a somewhat sarcastic voice) you just missed an opportunity to turn me into a loyal customer.

It's a shame that these aggressive, manipulative business techniques seem to be encroaching more and more onto the business scene. Because sales can be one of the noblest professions in the world. Sadly, salespeople get a bad rap for a few reasons: the person who misrepresents the product, the broken promises, and the failure to deliver what you said you would. There is also a prominent pushy, assuming communication style versus asking-us-permission style. However, being a successful salesperson does require polite persistence along with knowing when to stop, making marketing honorable and ethical. What could be finer than problem solving, showing affinity for your clients, and helping them live a better life by following their dreams to results?

I am interested in building "real-lationships." How about you?

Aren't you tired of the poor customer service that has permeated our country? Let's be real. At *least* half of all companies have poor customer care. Together, let's change all that. The word *relationship* is spoken of all the time—but have you taken the time to truly build a relationship with your prospective or current clients or customers? Dear readers, you know I like to create words.

"Real-lationships" is my word for partners and alliances that go beyond superficiality and immaturity to a quality and depth that enhances both your professional and personal life.

I am interested in building "real-lationships." How about you? According to *Merriam-Webster,* the word *relationship* means "the state of being related or connected." And I particularly love this definition: "the way in which two or more people, groups, countries, etc., talk to, behave toward, and deal with each other." Based on this, we could say we build good relationships or poor relationships. Relationships break down when we don't maintain respect or courtesy when interacting with others. You must learn to truly connect with others to build trust and sales. We're not a vendor; we're not a transaction but a living person with needs and heart and emotions.

Today's customers are really demanding. Our expectations are high. Great customer care has taught us that. I only got to fly Virgin America airlines once before they stopped flying from our local airport, but what an experience! First, they served Karma champagne—who's ever heard of a champagne called Karma? Second, the welcome from the crew was heartfelt. You could feel it. Third, the safety message was not the same old boring dialogue. This one was filled with wit and sarcasm. My feeling was that Virgin had a communication style that was funny and geared toward the passengers. I also felt that to Virgin, we were travelers first and customers second.

So let me ask you some key questions: What do you do better than anyone else? What problem have you solved in your own unique way unlike anybody else? How can you communicate in a voice that stands for your brand so you don't sound like everyone else?

I asked author Scott McKain about this issue. He is the founder of the Distinction Group, and he reveals that there are four keys to being distinctive. His expertise lies in helping clients create a brand that stands out in the marketplace. According to him, the four keys are:

1. Clarity

2. Creativity

3. Communication

4. Customer experience

Scott's fourth point is especially important for this chapter. He says this is emotional—in other words, how do I feel about being your customer? If there are seven dry cleaners in my community, the one

I will take my business to is the dry cleaner who makes me feel good as a customer. Speaking of clean clothes, let me tell you a story about a dry cleaner I recently encountered.

Six months ago I was seeking a new dry cleaner after moving to Monterey, California. I had seen the local newspaper's best-of-2020 edition, and I got very excited to see who'd won best dry cleaner. I gathered up my jacket, fancy dress, and all my hangers for reuse and loaded my car, keen to explore my new neighborhood. You know how it is when you move to a new location. You are eager to meet new folks and find local places to do business with. When I arrived, I saw a long line, but that didn't deter me. I thought, "Wow, this place must be even better than the reviews said." When I finally made it into the shop, one of the women motioned me over. She looked agitated, but I smiled warmly and said, "I just moved here, and I understand that you are the best dry cleaner in town." She barely looked up from her computer, seemed completely disinterested, did not smile, and replied in a matter-of-fact, flat voice, "Yeah, well, word of mouth." When folks show such a lack of warmth in customer relations, I have to admit I am always a little shocked. Like many women, I have been socialized to be nice and polite. Some of you might think I should have walked right out with my clothes, but I always like to give people a second chance.

Unfortunately, I never received the promised text message advising when my items would be ready for pick-up. So I randomly went back two weeks later hoping my clothes would be ready. They were ready, and my clothes looked really nice. But the cost was high, and the service was extremely low. Frankly, I don't enjoy paying that much for rude service! This establishment lost my business as I went in search of and found a new dry cleaner. My neighbor recommended a dry cleaner, saying that she had heard good things. My new dry cleaner is a family-run business, and the woman who runs the business quickly leaps up from her chair and greets me when I walk through the threshold. She always asks how I am or asks about the weather in a caring and friendly way.

Now that you have seen how *not* to do it—and since my book is all about showing more clarity, courtesy, kindness, and wisdom in the way we speak —consider this. I invite you to go and create your own unique voice/greeting/message that speaks to your ideal customer when they walk in, whether this is your store or your corporate office. Potential clients will be more likely to hear you and see you, and they get to embark on a customer experience that only you can craft.

> **My book is all about showing more clarity, courtesy, kindness, and wisdom in the way we speak.**

I'm going to share a story about exceptional customer experience. One word does make a difference. We'd recently returned to our former home in Silicon Valley and spent the weekend at Hotel Nia in Menlo Park, California. My husband and I were positively thrilled with their warm welcome and highly professional service. The hotel confirmation email said, "We look forward to greeting you soon." The typical email message you receive when booking reservations is "We look forward to seeing you soon." Almost all of the Hotel Nia personnel made it a point to warmly greet us each and every time we spoke (reinforcing their welcome email). The staff seemed to be exceptional at communication, especially the Friday night restaurant manager and the waitstaff. When you are made to feel like you matter with consistent attention paid to your needs, you will probably linger longer, order dessert, and maybe even have another adult beverage or cup of cappuccino. It's good for business. You will naturally spend more with a business that you like and trust, and of course we will return to this hotel.

I must say—that weekend we hit the jackpot for good service! My husband and I departed Menlo Park and drove north to Napa before heading back to our Monterey home. We stopped at one of the farm markets to get some fresh strawberries and honey. We were all properly wearing our masks, which makes it hard to understand what someone is saying, especially regarding numbers or amounts of money. I hear from my left ear, so I used to also read lips before the masks covered our mouths. The woman who assisted us said, "That will be sixteen dollars and fifty cents" and then showed us the total amount of the sale on her calculator. Brilliant! Simple! Now we have the visual to back up what we heard. You can make it easier for people to do business with you before you even say thank you.

Corporations could learn lessons from these smaller businesses. My feeling is that potential clients are more likely to want to embark on a customer experience journey with you if you have crafted that journey with special care. I know this might be hard for some of you, but let's talk about calling your phone company! Most people I know think that their phone company is the absolute worst at customer service. However, I believe *my* phone company's abysmal customer service is the worst.

After the third or fourth time of being transferred and still not being connected to the right person, I asked the agent, "Have you ever called yourself?" It was no surprise that her answer was no. If you are the boss of the phone company, do you seem to be wrapped up entirely in how things have always been done? Is your focus primarily on profits and employees to the point that you neglect your customers? Do I need to remind you that your customers make your business possible?

I keep my business with AT&T, because the network is solid in comparison to all the other carriers, but I would not increase my business or buy anything new from this particular phone company. And I absolutely dread when I have to call them.

For those of you who own a restaurant, this one's for you! When you walk into a restaurant, what usually falls out of the mouth of the host? "Hey, guys (don't get me started)!" or "Do you have reservations?" Boring. Expected. What if you heard this instead, "Are we expecting you this evening?" or "Good evening, have you reserved with us?" or "Welcome, how many are in your dining party tonight?" Can you feel the difference? Sometimes it seems like a surprise instead of a happy occurrence when we walk into an establishment. Restaurateurs, please train your hosts, for they are the first point of contact and their communication makes a very strong impression on us.

Another reason to participate in what I call smart-heart communication is the millions of dollars it costs companies each year because of ineffective, sloppy communication. I mean, we've got the murky talk, the employees who don't say what they mean, and the lack of follow-up and follow-through on promises and deliverables. Folks, it costs you hundreds of thousands, perhaps millions, to not address and fix communication problems. When hiring your customer service team, those who are the first-line representatives of your company, hire people who have a heart to serve. Hire those folks who think it is an honor to serve others and solve problems. You can train them to do the rest if this basic value and attitude are solidly in place and part of who they are. Train them well, and give them ownership, meaning the authority to make it right for the

> No, the customer is not always right, but you can make it right for the customer.

customer. No, the customer is not always right, but you can make it right for the customer.

In fact, you never know where your next business might come from. It is smart to be kind to all folks because, after all, they could end up hiring you. I was once hired from a conversation in a supermarket just because I was wearing a sweatshirt that advertised a jazz festival. The man questioned me about my sweatshirt, thinking that I could help his wife with her voice. He ended up becoming a client. You never know what magic will come into your life when you are paying attention and take a moment to talk. Keep your mind and heart receptive to possibility and potential.

And if you are a man, don't fall into what I call the "I'm the man" syndrome, something that I became aware of just recently (yes, this is my work too) while having telephone conversations with two different men. I was asking for some type of insight or asking them what their opinion was, and they both responded with "I can't tell you what to do." This must be some type of automatic response from alpha males. I didn't ask you to tell me what to do—why did you make that assumption? I was seeking to understand more or learn or discover a better solution for myself and my life. What you would do is probably not what I would do anyway. The point is to offer intelligent advice if you can. Respectful responding would be the mature and evolved way of answering someone even if you don't have another interaction with the person. The one man was a lawyer, and if I needed a lawyer, do you think I would ever go to him? No, and he missed the entire opportunity because he treated our entire conversation as a phone call he was most anxious to leave, from clearing his throat repeatedly in my ear to a decided lack of interest in my questions.

Finally, I encourage you to concentrate on how you will make more sales by simply creating an amazing customer experience for us. Why not make it fun, like a game? Think of most stores. When you walk into a store, the person typically greets you with, "Hi, can I help you?" And most people will say "no," which is a missed opportunity. Instead, I propose the following: "Welcome, what may I show you today?" or "What may I help you find today?"

You have no idea if the person walking in has an American Express black card or Venmo just begging to be used. You can't tell whether someone has money or whether they will spend it. Never assume, but instead anticipate that you as a sales associate will have a great time working with us. Show us some love, show us you care, keep your language specific, and actively invite us to a shopping experience with open-ended questions.

I feel my book would not be complete without a discussion of value-based pricing. When I started my business, I charged by the hour and attracted every tire kicker and cheapskate (a person who is unwilling to spend money) possible. It was a big mistake.

I draw from my peer Ronald J. Baker, who is a CPA, the author of several books, and the founder of VeraSage Institute. For those of you who have ever resented the price you paid for by-the-hour work or if you are a professional who charges by the hour, I urge you to consider pricing on value.

Here is what he shared with me in his words:

> "Any company that establishes prices based upon value will agree that the conversation with the customer is the most important part of the process. Skipping an in-depth conversation is similar to a contractor attempting to build a customer's dream home without any architectural plans. The better your firm *comprehends* the customer's value drivers, the more likely you will be able to *create* maximum value, *convince* the customer they must pay for that value,

and *capture* a fair portion of that value with an effective pricing strategy custom tailored to the customer."

This is an opportunity for you and the customer to create a shared vision of the future, to analyze where the customer is at this point, and to develop the necessary action plan to move them to where they want to be. It is a transformation, and when you offer personalized and customized transformations, the customer is the product.

This focus is crucial because if you do not discuss value with the customer, you will be forced into a discussion of hours, efforts, activities, deliverables, and costs, usually by procurement, in-house counsel, or some other professional buyer within the customer's organization. Remember that the customer is trying to *maximize* the value they receive while attempting to *minimize* your price. It is far more strategic to engage in a discussion over what the customer is trying to maximize rather than what they are trying to minimize. If all you focus on is price, it can never be low enough. If the customer says your price is too high, what they are really saying is, "I don't see the value in your offering." It is not a question of money; rather, it is lack of belief.

> **It is not a question of money; rather, it is lack of belief.**

This is one of the most effective statements to use somewhere near the beginning of the conversation, regardless of whether you are meeting with a new or current client:

"Ms. Client, we will only undertake this project if we can agree, to our mutual satisfaction, that the value we are creating is at least three (to ten) times the price we are charging you. Is that acceptable?"

Do not get sidetracked by the multiple of three to ten, as it will obviously vary from customer to customer. In fact, sometimes you do not need to state a multiple, rather just state that the value needs to exceed the price.

This establishes the right tone near the beginning of the conversation, demonstrating yours is a firm obsessed with value and showing the economic impact that your services can have for the customer—how your services will improve the customer's life. It also subtly suggests that you will not enter into relationships that do not add value for both parties—the exact tone you want to set, as both sides to a transaction must profit if it is to be sustainable.

And I will close the pricing discussion with what I consider Ron's most profound words, "There is great nobility in getting paid what you are worth. Nothing is more satisfying than customers who believe—and act on the premise—that they get what they pay for. The best way to achieve this is to have a value conversation."

Make it easy to do business with you!

Please, please, please (is that enough?)—make it easy to do business with you!

Begin to think of yourself as always being your own best brand ambassador. You are the sales representative as you show up in the world. You are also the voice of your company, and your reputation is everything. Showing up with clear, courteous communication and presence will always pay off in some way whether you know it or not. You cannot control how a message is received by the other party, but you can completely stack the deck in your favor by communicating with a clear, concise, compassionate, and inclusive message that is more likely to land beautifully.

And, finally, *ask* for the sale. Yes, ask. If you have had adequate conversations and established your credibility and the other person truly would benefit from your product or service, then why would you not make an offer to work with them? Wouldn't that be the very definition of an honorable exchange? Travel back to when you were a little kid who was not the least bit afraid of asking (and begging and negotiating) for what you wanted? Don't change your voice tone; don't get all weird; simply ask for the business. Ask for the sale, and then be quiet.

Three Ways to Have a Better Sales Conversation In Person or Virtually

1. Selling doesn't have to be stressful. Make it fun by using your own unique way of selling favoring your personality. We have all had the experience of unpleasant haggling or feeling "beat up" by a salesperson who was taught to dominate us or denigrate the competition. Why would you even draw attention to any competition by mentioning it? Know your product or service, stay in your lane, and do what you do best by serving as a trusted guide no matter what you're selling.

2. If you are team presenting or selling, set up your chairs side by side (when in person) or closely matching on video. Prepare your backdrop. Set up your camera so that you are viewed from the upper chest and above, with the focus on your head and eyes. Set up a practice view beforehand. Ensure that the size of each person is closely matching and that any distractions are removed from the background. Check your microphone and sound level— is each one of you equally well heard?

3. Present your findings, pitch your pitch, or make your sales presentation. Then be ready to actively listen. Remember, the "other" part of the communication exchange is listening. As people begin to drop their resistance and defenses, they will reveal more about what they really want. Then you will know if you hit the mark or not, and it is so much easier to course correct and add value with additional information.

Folks, we are nearing the end of my book. Up next is the grand finale, the encore containing deep thoughts, my Top Ten Miluna-isms to inspire you, and an invitation.

What Is Your Pitch-Perfect Voice and Speech?

Wow—you did it! You read my book. And I trust my book changed the way you think about your voice, communication, and professional presence forever.

Here's my in-your-face question: Do you want to continue as mediocre man or what-happened woman? People—it's time to get off your comfort couch! The leaders we will be looking up to will speak with intelligence and heart, compassion and courage. If you choose to begin to speak differently, it will lead directly to a better quality of life and relationships. I promise—you can ask my clients.

I encourage you to begin to craft a different way of speaking. Your voice matters—we need you. You use your voice when speaking and writing. The voice is our original instrument; it came with you! This also means that you can change and grow your voice, personal expression, and leadership abilities just like any other self-growth or training you invest in. You can reinvent and re-create yourself and the way you express yourself at any time.

Mind your words. Your words matter. In the shamanic traditions that have been practiced on our planet for over one hundred thousand years, your words are, indeed, magic.

Mind your delivery. Your delivery matters. What the world needs now is respectful, inclusive communication. Civil debates. We must cultivate an ability to disagree without shaming or dominating others with an opinion. We must disagree without being disagreeable.

It has been a privilege and a pleasure to have you here with me, and I am humbled that you have read my book.

I will close and leave you now with my Top Ten Miluna-isms. Remember, my door is open and I'll leave the light on for you!

My Top Ten Miluna-isms for Life (So Far)

1. I encourage you to be a creative genius: ponder, play, create new words, change your name, take a different route to work, wear a new watch, and decide where and with whom to spend your time, energy, love, and money.

2. FOOPO—fear of other people's opinions will make you fearful, weary, and sad. Learn to hear and listen to your own voice. You must be present to your life. Ditch FOOPO!

3. Practice means prepared and professional (PP&P).

4. Any deep transformation involves healing and takes time. It is worth it to set yourself apart by training to be a confident, dynamic, effective speaker and world-class presenter.

5. Walk your talk. Don't just talk and talk.

6. When you get to that fork in the road—choose the road that excites that little child within you!

7. If you know how, then your "what" is not big enough! You must speak your dreams aloud with affirmations and take action first to uncover and discover who you really are.

8. Cultivate true friendships with those folks who are big enough to get you and love you, tell you the truth (kindly), and hold your dreams in their heart.

9. If you've been called too much, too different, too sensitive, or too caring—you're on the right path to being true to who you are.

10. Recognize when others are trying to take your power. Set what I call a "love boundary"; communicate clearly, and don't allow it. Go within, not with-out.

Be a Part of the Exclusive World of "When You Care Enough to Speak the Very Best"

This is your invitation to join the movement and help restore civil, respectful, clear, and beautiful language to our society. Now is the perfect time to evolve.

If I can help you, do speak up and contact me. I invite you to reach out and join my Pitch Perfect Insiders, easy to do at https://www.MilunaFausch.com/. When you join, twice a month you will receive video tips and first notice of events and UpLevel Your Communication mastermind groups.

You may also choose to join an *UpLevel Your Communication* book club/mastermind. Sign up here:

https://www.milunafausch.com/uplevelyourcommunication

About the Author

Dr. Miluna Fausch
Photo by Mark Maryanovich, Los Angeles

Miluna Fausch has an intuitive and scientific problem-solving perspective coming from a multipassionate experience working nine-to-fives, in retail, and as an entrepreneur, serving on nonprofit boards, and performing on stage and screen. She has sold everything from magazine advertisements to Steinway grand pianos. Dr. Miluna is an intuitive sound healer who helps others through sounds, words, and music.

Dr. Miluna has a bachelor of science degree in music business, is a certified holistic health counselor practitioner, has a PhD in holistic psychology, and has extensive training in voice, acting, energy healing, and intuition in addition to being certified as a Miracle-Minded

Coach by Marianne Williamson. Dr. Miluna created her proprietary Vocal Archetypes^{sm} system to train conscientious C-suite executives and thought leaders in confident and compelling communication, voice, and presence.

In her free time, she can be found attending concerts and lectures, traveling, wine tasting, watching Formula 1 auto races, doing her best to avoid eating a whole bag of jelly beans, serving on the advisory board of Love Never Fails, and serving as a college mentor with Mountain View and Los Altos (MVLA) Scholars.

Dr. Miluna and her husband, Reto, make their home in Monterey, California.

www.ingramcontent.com/pod-product-compliance
Lightning Source LLC
Chambersburg PA
CBHW050528190326
41458CB00045B/6743/J